PRINCIPLES OF
SELF-GOVERNANCE

Solution to the Current Global Political,
Economic, and Social Crises

ABRAHAM JOHN

Principles of Self-Governance: Solutions to Current Global Political, Economic and Social Crises

Healing of the Nations Series 1

Copyright © 2025 by Abraham John

Published by Abraham John
For the Tree of Life
www.TheKingdomNetwork.org
email: mim@maximpact.org

1 800 558 5020
(720) 560 4664

ISBN: 978-1-948330-36-7

Published in the United States of America

Unless otherwise indicated, all Scripture taken from the New King James Version®. Copyright © 1982 by Thomas Nelson. Used by permission.

Scripture marked (KJV) is from the King James Version of the Bible, which is in the public domain.

Scripture marked (AMP) is from The AMPLIFIED BIBLE. 1982. Zondervan Bible Publishers, Grand Rapids, Michigan, USA

All *emphasis* or additions in parentheses within scriptural quotations are the author's own.

All rights reserved. No part of this book may be reproduced or transmitted in any form or by any means, electronic or mechanical, including photocopying, recording, or by any information storage and retrieval system, without permission in writing from the author. Please direct your inquiries to mim@maximpact.org

Table of Contents

Preface	7
Introduction	15
Chapter 1 Self-Awareness	19
Chapter 2 What is Self-Awareness?	41
Chapter 3 Leaving Your *Chicken Coop*	*71*
Chapter 4 Self-Discovery	91
Chapter 5 Self-Empowerment	117
Chapter 6 Self-Actualization	143
Chapter 7 Self-Government	157
Bibliography and Recommended Resources	179

How to use this book to get the best out of it?

This is a Handbook for Life. It is not an ordinary book that you will read, discard, and then simply forget about it all.

This book was specifically designed in an interactive style. Every chapter has questions designed to help you locate where you are in the process of fulfilling your purpose.

The more you interact and invest your time to study and apply the principles mentioned in this book, the more benefit you will receive from this interaction.

Please, don't treat this as a normal book. Keep it and take it with you wherever you go. Read it again and again, while tracking the progress you make. Keep this book until your deathbed, and then hand it over to the next generation.

Welcome to the process of healing the nations.

Preface

Why Self Governance?

There are more failed states and economies today than ever in human history. Every day we hear about wars and instability. Governments are running out of solutions for their citizens and for their respective countries. People everywhere are looking for answers and solutions. They can't find any. Christians who were told Jesus is the answer, but feel as lost as anyone else out there in the world.

Imagine close to a million government employees getting fired from their jobs in one day. Or, imagine the cash in your bank account being declared invalid. Imagine millions of people being deported as illegal immigrants; or stuck in refugee camps.

Governments reach their debt ceiling every few months because of overspending and mismanagement. We have tested and tried various forms of governments.

Why is every form of government and other institutions failing on the earth?

I read in the news the other day, that people everywhere are leaning toward more authoritarian forms of government; mainly, because they believe stricter rules and regulations will solve their problems, and because of the failures and injustices previous governments inflicted upon their citizens. Fear is the number one tactic to gain control over people's minds.

Do you know that human beings were not created to be governed externally by enforcing laws or rules over them? This may be shocking news to you. While such governance may work for a season, the people will eventually rebel, and then that system will collapse and fall. How many stories of revolutions, collapsed empires, kingdoms and failed governments do we read of in our history books?

The more laws we try to enforce, the more breaking of laws will occur. Enforcing stricter laws are not permanent solutions to any social or political problems.

How did God Almighty plan to govern the affairs of the earth and human beings?

What type of government did He have in mind?

We were created to be governed from *within*—governed by the *God-factor* within each one of us. We were born free. Freedom is the greatest gift the Creator gave to each individual.

When we surrender that freedom to another individual or to a government or an organization, we are going against our very own nature. We were not created to be enslaved or dominated by anyone. We were created in the image and likeness of God. This means we were created to function like God functions.

When God created the first human being, He did not give him any laws, rules, or regulations. All He told him was, not to eat the fruit of a particular tree. Everything else He told him and set in place was to empower Adam for *self-governance*, in order to fulfill his destiny.

Why was Adam not eating from the fruit of a particular tree such a big deal to God?[1]

---

[1] To know more about this please read What Happened to God book. www.TheKingdomNetwork.org

Preface

The ancient kingdom of Israel came to their prophet at that time, and said, "Give us a king like other nations" (1 Samuel 8:5-6). What they were basically saying was, we don't want to take responsibility to govern ourselves; we want someone else to rule over us, and tell us what to do. We want a king to tell us when to go out and when to come in. We are willing to abdicate our wills and freedom to this king, and do what he says.

That was the second biggest mistake next to Adam eating from the wrong tree, and saying to God, we don't want to be self-governed under Your rulership, but we want to be governed by a system of good and evil.

It was both the saddest day and a turning point in the history of Israel. God gave them a king, and that king failed his people and God miserably. That kingdom of Israel only lasted for two generations, then it collapsed. They never fully recovered from that fall, to this day.

How many failed governments have we witnessed in our lifetime?

Every few years, we keep electing a new leader—thinking that he or she is going to get everything right, and solve the age-old problems for us—only to find that they couldn't deliver on what they promised. And so, we start looking for the next person, while the person we elected previously is still in the office; who again says what we want to hear, and we go through the same cycle yet again.

We thought democracy was better than communism. But if we really examine democracy, it is failing faster than we can stop or control it. The main reason for this is corruption, and it is not a God-ordained system. Democracy gives us an opportunity to work toward the goal of self-governance. If we don't make that transition, democracy won't last.

The government of our day is a system that is set up and run by people. If any system is corrupted, that means there are corrupt people behind it. Any new system or product we invent, we end up using them to do more evil than good with it.

Principles of Self Governance

The purpose of government is not to rule over people by inflicting fear or control, but to empower and support people to govern themselves; to establish a system where every citizen is empowered and free to fulfill their God-given purpose; to come alongside and make sure every system and process is running smoothly, and to provide each individual with the tools and support they need.

In every human being, there is a divine dissatisfaction with the government of their country. No earthly form of government will satisfy this longing. Only when we discover and implement the government God envisioned for us, will we feel safe, have our expectations satisfied, and our freedom secured.

People in every country are more divided than ever. Religious extremism, liberalism, racism, conservatism, economic division, and gender confusion are some of the factors that divide people into various groups; and sometimes cause them to hate and fight each other.

People are becoming less and less interested in religions as a whole. We were not created for any religion. Religions are failing to provide real answers to real problems and questions human beings have. Therefore, many don't want anything to do with religion or God anymore.

Church buildings and cathedrals are lying empty in almost every city. We were created for a relationship with God Almighty. We turned that relationship into a bunch of rituals and institutions. God wants us to relate with Him as His children. He doesn't want any rituals, regulations or mediators.

Non-governmental organizations are failing and running out of resources. The need is so great, the more they try to solve these, new ones emerge.

Educational systems are failing to produce responsible citizens. Universities and colleges have become the corridor for political and

Preface

radical indoctrination, instead of empowering an individual to reach self-discovery.

In some countries, it takes a bag full of cash to buy a loaf of bread.

We keep looking for solutions outside of ourselves. We keep looking for this superhuman being to suddenly appear from nowhere and solve all the problems for us.

What we don't realize is that each one of us is that superhuman put here by God. Any human being in whom God Almighty dwells, becomes superhuman. The solution to the problems we face in our world today are waiting to be discovered inside each one of us. We were sent here to solve a problem. What we need is *self-discovery*, not more rules.

People don't have time to stop and think about life—why they are alive, and why they are doing what they are doing—they are bogged down by the responsibilities of life, and trying to survive. They are chasing this mirage, only to find out what they were chasing all their life, was not somewhere out there; it was lying dormant inside them, all along.

Most people wait for someone else to come and discover their greatness, cheer them up, and lead them by their hands. We want people to rally behind what we know and believe; and support our mission in life. The problem is, unfortunately those people never show up.

We hide the treasure that is inside us, mainly because of fear and self-doubt; and as a result, we fail to recognize the value of what we carry. What nobody told us, is that those people will only come after we let the light that is inside us shine. The brighter we shine it, the more people it will attract.

Each one of us carries a treasure inside us. This treasure is called *the kingdom of heaven*. It is made of righteousness, peace and joy. It contains the government that we are longing for, the solutions to every problem

Principles of Self Governance

we face in life. And, once we discover and manifest it, everything we need in life will be added to us or will come to us.

The longer we wait and look for someone to come and save us, the more we waste and let others squander our resources and time. Others are merely waiting to disappear from the earth, because they don't know what to do with the mess they find around them.

I want to present to you a better way and a better form of government. It is called *self-governance*. It is an ancient way that our Creator envisioned for us to be governed by Him.

In most countries governments consume the lion's share of the budget and resources. If we follow the system of self-governance, we can cut some ninety-percent of government spending. There won't be any crime in our streets. Everyone will live in peace, love and in harmony.

We won't need to spend any money manufacturing weapons to kill people. There won't be any need for wars. The proportion of the money countries spend on their defense budgets to protect themselves and to kill their enemies, alone, will be enough to eradicate poverty from the earth.

We won't need any prisons. We won't need any religions or politicians. We won't need any religious institutions. Everyone will become one with God and with each other.

If we follow self-governance and its principles, we can get rid of all sicknesses and diseases, thus eventually getting rid of all the hospitals.

Imagine how much money and wealth we would save? We could then use all of that for development and conservation. There won't be any drug cartels or gangs. There won't be any poor or anyone with an unmet need. There won't be any illegal immigration problems or refugee camps. There won't be any human or sex trafficking.

I am inviting my fellow human beings to try this system of self-governance and see whether it will work. Many of you reading this

Preface

book may already be functioning in this system, unaware. Even though you are living in a country with a certain type of government oversight; personally, you have arrived at a place of self-governance. You are not waiting for someone to tell you what to do or how to live.

By the grace that is given to me, via this book I am going to explain about this simple way of governing our lives; which in turn will solve the political, economic and social crises we face in life and the world around us. Welcome to the journey of self-governance.

Introduction

This book will make the job of governments, churches, and other organizations and what they are striving to achieve in their countries, much easier.

There is a reason why every form of government and economy is failing. The number one reason why is, they are all fake. None of them are real.

The paper money that you hold in your hands and that you worked so hard for, is fake. Nobody in their right mind would pay that amount for a small piece of paper of that size. We assume that a small piece of paper or plastic has value because someone convinced us it is so valuable.

Imagine if you landed on a different planet where you picked up a piece of stone. You don't value that stone, as for you, it is just a stone. But, what if for those inhabitants who live on that planet, it could be the most costliest or precious stone. As long as you don't know about it, you won't know the value of it.

Imagine an alien landing in New York city and picking up a 100-dollar bill. That alien would not recognize the value of that piece of paper as we do. He may merely toss it and walk away.

Everything in life works the same way. What we think is important and valuable, may not be important and valuable to someone else.

Why is there no mention of any type of government in the book of Genesis?

The Bible says "the government shall be upon His shoulder." But it doesn't specify what type of government. We know that our God or Jesus is King, so it should be a Monarchy. But how did He plan to rule the whole world?

We all carry a God-factor inside us or a God Positioning System (GPS)—because we are all created in the image and likeness of God.

Many Christians believe Jesus is going to come back and set up His throne in Jerusalem to rule the whole world. How is He going to govern someone in Argentina or on the Island of Fiji, if He is only going to be in Jerusalem?

We believe Jesus lives inside us—Christ in us the hope of glory. If Jesus comes in person, will He leave us or stop living inside each believer? I don't think so. As He is now, so are we in this world. We are supposed to be the exact representation of the resurrected Christ right now on this earth.

By the end of the book you will come to your own conclusion whether this is practical or not. If you believe this is practical, let us connect and do something about this together, rather than waiting and wasting another lifetime.

You will find more information about what to do next, at the end of this book.

What is Self-Governance?

You may not have heard the term *self-governance* mentioned before. Although this exact term is not used in the Bible, we do see similar terms like *self-control* mentioned as part of the fruit of the spirit, while the New International Version (NIV) expresses this as *self-discipline*. Self-governance is a synonym for self-control and self-discipline.

Introduction

Imagine a country without unemployment, where everyone is fulfilling their God-given purpose. Every citizen becomes productive, contributing their equal and fair share in a society where people are not treated based on their income or class statuses, but based on their respective callings and the contributions they make.

Self-governance happens when each individual reaches a certain level of maturity, managed from within through the God-factor which is inside them, without any outside force or entity telling them what to do or what not to do. When people are self-managed by the God-factor that is within them, self-governance occurs.

Imagine a community or society without crime, prisons, corruption, hospitals, or any religion—where citizens live in peace, love, and in harmony with one another and nature. This is possible, however, this can only be achieved through self-governance.

How is self-governance achieved?

This happens through empowering each Individual to reach a place of

Self-awareness

which leads to

Self-discovery

which leads to

Self-empowerment

which leads to

Self-actualization

which leads to

Self-governance

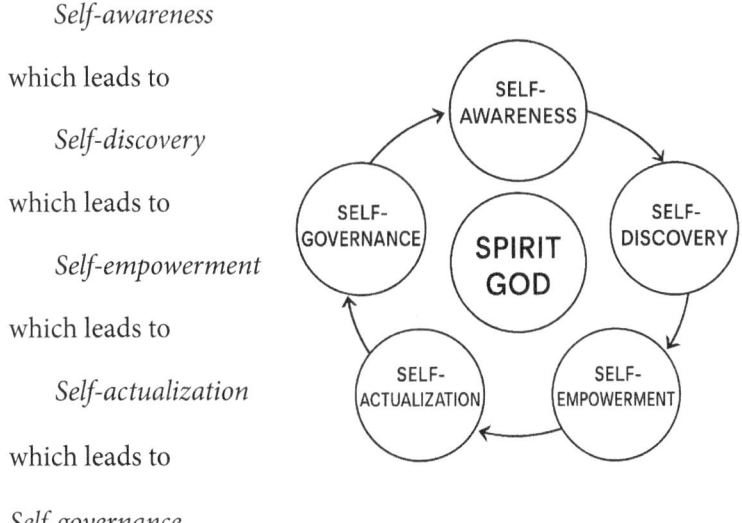

- **Self-awareness** is realizing who we are—waking up to our true selves and identity

- **Self-discovery** is discovering our purpose, potential, and possibilities—which leads to self-empowerment

- **Self-empowerment** is when an individual accepts personal responsibility for where they are currently in life, and intentionally cultivates habits and interests in order to learn, grow, and attain the next level in life.

Which leads to **self-actualization**, where each one manifests their potential and gifts, by identifying, utilizing, and maximizing the resources and opportunities that are available—thus becoming a responsible and productive citizen.

Which, in turn, leads to **self-governance**, where each one is fulfilling their God-given purpose, by creating an environment for everyone around them to live in love, peace, and in harmony; making wise choices based on their mature spirit; and finally leaving a legacy for future generations to do the same.

They are governed from within. This should be the purpose of all education and governments. Let us explore each of these steps a bit further.

This book has a dual purpose and meanings for everything that is written in it:

- The first one, is to know where each one of us are in relation to reaching self-governance.

- The second one is when you read, you will see yourself in the lines as if you are looking in a mirror.

This book is a reflection of yourself. Welcome to the journey of self-governance.

CHAPTER 1

Self-Awareness

You may be wondering *why a book about "self?"*—when we were taught all our lives, self is evil and the problem, and our goal is to get rid of it. Some believe that when we are able to get rid of the self, then we shall achieve some level of true spirituality or holiness. That is not true.

Before we delve into self-awareness, let me share a little bit about self-denial first.

Self-denial

Many people grew up in different religions and heard different teachings on *self*. Many misunderstood the verse where Jesus mentioned *denying our self* or *dying to self*.

They think that self-denial means becoming a monk or a nun or to lead an ascetic life. Others feel there is something wrong with themselves, and so, now they need to deny it or reject themselves. So they live in self-rejection, which robs them of their productivity and effectiveness. That is not what Jesus meant when He said to deny ourselves (Luke 9:23).

The problem each one of us face is not with our true self, but the fake personas and false selves or identities. What Jesus meant was to deny the false or fake self that we built up, or the one that was put onto us while we were growing up—which hinders us from being real and from living an authentic life.

So, it's the self that was formed by the *chicken coop* that we were raised up in, which formed a false and fake identity about ourselves, that self needs to be denied or surrendered. This is self-denial.

The self that Jesus wanted us to deny is the one that stands between us and Him, between us and our purpose, between us and our authentic selves which steals the joy of living and adds unnecessary miseries. This is the *ego* that blocks His love and kingdom from being manifested in and from flowing through us; the self that makes us self-reliable rather than relying on Him and His grace. The fake self hinders us from having meaningful and fulfilling relationships—that self must go.

Jesus told us to love our neighbor as we love ourselves. Why is it so difficult for us to love our neighbor? We preach about it, but how many of us truly practice it? If we don't love our true selves, then we can't love our neighbor. The reason why many of us are not able to love our neighbor as we love ourselves, is because we are in love with our fake selves, which causes selfishness; which leads to self-preservation, and creates wrong perceptions of ourselves and others.

We don't want anyone to find that fake self, so we go into hiding, pretending or self-absorption. Then, we end up building walls around our hearts first, then around our properties, and then around our communities; instead of building bridges. Unless we unravel that which is false and fake, we will never discover the true and authentic.

Loving our True Selves and our Neighbors

Self in itself, is not evil. People go to work every day in order to take care of themselves. Jesus wants us to love the real self, not deny it. Many of our problems are rooted in lack of self love.

Chapter 1 | Self-Awareness

There is a difference between self love and selfishness. Selfishness is self centered. Self love emanates from knowing God loved us first. Once we are aware of that then we are able to love ourselves and others with the same love.

When we go through the process mentioned in this book to understand the difference between fake and true self, we can identify who we really are; and in turn, identify who our neighbor is, and love them for where they are at. True love changes people—not rules and walls.

One of the best things we could achieve and live by, is having a true and authentic self. This is one of the greatest blessings anyone could achieve and then share it with their fellow human beings. If we do, we can solve almost all the problems we face in this world. That is what this book is about.

Self in itself is not evil. God created our *self*. However, something happened to us, as there is a certain amount of "fakeness" or "weirdness" in all of us which we don't want others to know about or discover.

Fake selves

In trying to hide that weirdness from others, we ended up building this fake *self* as we tried to protect ourselves. As a result, our purpose and destinies were stripped from us.

We used different ingredients to build that fake self. Some used religion, others culture, race, education, profession, money, skills, nationality, etc. As a result, the people and nations that were supposed to benefit from us by fulfilling our destinies, remain in need.

From the time we wake up until we go to bed we are dealing with our *self*. How is self a bad thing when we are aware of it and take care of it 24/7? What we do with that self, and how we live, is what truly matters. This is why self-awareness is so important.

Self-awareness

The human race waited four thousand years for their Messiah to come. When He came, He told us not to join any religion or to add any new religious rituals, or to build more synagogues.

The first thing He told us was to "repent." Repent doesn't mean to feel sorry for what we did, or to feel bad for what happened to us or go to church or temples on Sundays. *Repent* means to come to self-awareness and know who you are, what happened to you, and why you are doing what you are doing; and make a U-turn. He wants us to discover and deal with the root, instead of the fruit.

It doesn't matter what God can do or has made available to us, or planned for us. Until we step out and "do it," nothing happens. Religious people flippantly say "God is in control" or "God is going to do it." If that were true, why then is this world in such a mess, and why hasn't He fixed it yet?

This is why "self" is very important. For thousands of years, God Almighty has been waiting for each one of us to get to a place of self-awareness.

True repentance is all about self-awareness. When we look at life from God's perspective, repentance begins. We will feel sorry, guilty, and bad for where we are and what we did compared to what God wanted. When repentance happens, we realize *who* we are, *how* we reached where we are, *what* happened to us in the process; and the course correction that needs to take place, and then finally receive the roadmap for how we reach our destination.

Whatever is hindering us from living and experiencing the life God wants us to have, is because of the false and fake *self*. It could be various masks we are wearing and hiding behind, or a false image we built up about ourselves. It could be a religious image or titles, positions, tradition, belief systems, mistakes, regrets, ego, or emotional wounds, etc.

When we deny our false or fake self, it will generate a certain amount of suffering and we could face persecution; that is the cross Jesus told us to carry. The cross represents suffering. When we decide to be real and live an authentic life, people who are still living in their fake or false self will misunderstand and try to misjudge us. That generates persecution.

Even Jesus, the perfect and sinless Messiah was misunderstood by the majority of the people, particularly by those who claimed to be holy and most spiritual. They accused Him of being demon-possessed. Imagine that.

My attempt with this chapter is to help us identify that false *self* we inherited. None of us are exempt from this. Because their current identity, belief systems, sometimes even livelihood, and their whole life could be built upon it; only a few are willing to recognize it, and then deal with it.

Defining Who We Really Are

Most people live and die without ever realizing *who* they really are. Others live and die without ever knowing *why* they were born—their purpose. If you had asked them the question, "Who are you?" they would have answered "I am Robert," or "I am Lily" "I am an American," or "I am an Indian," or even, "I am a doctor," or "I am a businessman" or "I am a businesswoman," "sales person;" or even, "I am a Christian," or "I am a Hindu."

The truth is, none of their answers reveal who these people really are. Their answers are about their names, nationality, their jobs or profession, their religious or church affiliation; which were given to them after they were born.

The truth is, before they were identified or defined by their nationality, names, race, jobs, or religion, they already existed.

How then do we define a person without names, nationality, skills, political, gender, race, jobs and religious affiliation?

When a person is able to define themselves and their identity apart from their nationality, names, jobs, skills, race, gender, political or religious affiliation; that person has reached a state of *self-awareness*. They are able to detect that there is something more to life than merely what they were taught, had known or were doing. They may not fully understand everything, but there is a divine dissatisfaction deep down within their being. They may not know how to explain it, but it's there.

Before We Were Born

The truth is, everything most people say regarding their identity was imposed on them or was taught them since birth. They don't realize they existed before they were born.

We are spirit-beings sent from a faraway kingdom to accomplish something for that King and His kingdom on the earth. We will discuss this further later on.

The number one key to live a meaningful and successful life on the earth is to have self-awareness. Most people don't get to live their life, or the true version of themselves, but only get to live someone else's idea or definition of what life is; or the definition of the religion they are part of. So, they choose the path of least resistance as part of the crowd. Most follow the crowd, they do something because everybody around them is doing it.

The majority don't know why they are here. They just keep on doing the same old thing, and never bother to stop to ask for directions. Some are bold enough to question their current reality, but only a few find the answers. Even fewer are bold enough to do anything with the answers they find.

'Chicken coops' of culture, race, religion, nationality, broken families, etc

I remember the story of an eagle which was accidentally hatched out by a hen:

Chapter 1 | Self-Awareness

> The eaglet was born and was walking around with other chicks looking for worms and insects. The more it grew, the more it felt like it didn't belong in the chicken coop. Worms, insects and grains did not taste right. But it did not know what to do or who to ask for help. The mother chicken did not realize that she was raising an eaglet either.
>
> The mother chicken continued to encourage the eaglet to be like other chickens and do everything like the other chickens did—scratch on the ground, swallow the insects, and look at the ground when you walk. But the more the eaglet tried to fit in, the more discomfort it felt. Deep down inside, the eaglet knew that there was something wrong with this "life" in this chicken coop.

What most of us think is normal in life, is not supposed to be normal. This is how the eaglet's story continued to unfold:

> The mother chicken often scolded the eaglet, "Don't try to be different. When you grow up and lay eggs for your master, he will be happy, so you don't need to worry about your food or survival. You are safe in this chicken coop, as long as you stay here and do what everybody else does, and lay eggs; but if you try to go outside, it could be dangerous."

Do you feel like that eaglet? What you eat and where you live and what you do doesn't seem right. You feel like you were meant for more. You were made to do something unique and different.

We are all like that eaglet. We were sent from heaven to earth. But when we were born, we were all born into different *chicken coops*, Chicken coops of culture, race, religion, nationality, broken families, etc. We were taught to live like the other 'chickens,' our identity and purpose and worth were compromised. False and fake selves were imposed on us. We started to repeat what everybody around us was saying or doing. We thought this was all normal.

The only difference is, each of our 'chicken coops' were different. Some of us were born into different political ideologies, and that became our 'chicken coop' identity. Others were born into different religions and denominations, which became their 'chicken coop.' We were born into different countries and families. For others the abuses they had to endure became their 'chicken coop.' Whatever we are passionate about and identify ourselves with, or feel stuck with—apart from God and what He meant for us to be—is our personal 'chicken coop.'

We can't see beyond our 'chicken coops.' We define life and the world around us based on that 'coop' and our experience in it. We value people and things based on the environment we were brought up in. We were told that if we try to do anything different or think differently than what we were taught growing up in the 'chicken coop,' we would be considered a rebel or a backslider, or even an infidel.

To appease others and for the fear of rejection by others and their opinions, we sacrificed our true identity and purpose at the altars of those 'chicken coops.' By the time we realize what really happened, it could be too late for most people to do anything about it.

I don't want that to happen to you. This is why you are reading this book.

This is how the story of the eagle all played out:

> One day that eagle looked up, and saw something flying close to the clouds up in the sky. It never saw anything like that before. It was taught all its life to look to the ground and not to the sky. It thought everything with wings was supposed to be inside a chicken coop somewhere. That is what it was taught by the mother hen.
>
> The wind began to blow, and the storm raged. But it saw that a bird was soaring above the clouds through the storm.

Chapter 1 | Self-Awareness

Something inside that eagle said, "You can also do that, if you want to." However, it tried to talk itself out of it because it had never tried doing anything different, and consequently never believed it could fly. All it was taught in that coop was to think and live like a chicken. Anything beyond that was considered "impossible" or "out of boundary."

It couldn't take its eyes off that eagle flying in the sky. Something resonated inside him that challenged what was taught him to think like a chicken all its life. Other chickens next to it were resting and taking their afternoon naps. They had no idea what was happening inside their 'sibling.'

That day a seed of possibility was birthed inside that eagle. What if I try to fly? What if I try and fail and fall and hit the wall, or fall into a well? That would be the end of my life!

That is the language of fear.

The next day the same thing happened. It saw other eagles flying up in the sky and enjoying life without any restrictions. Something leaped inside its being as its natural instinct kicked in. Spontaneously, its wings flapped—an authentic response to its natural instinct fired by seeing another doing what it was born to do.

However, that flapping woke up all the chickens napping around that eagle. They were upset because it disturbed their afternoon nap, and created chaos inside the coop that was so peaceful.

The mother hen noticed what was happening, and started to rebuke the eagle for what it did. It said, "Why are you trying to be different? Everyone else here is happy and content for where and how life is. Why can't you be grateful for what you have, and settle where you are, and live like everybody else?"

The eagle felt guilty and bad for what just happened. It looked around and noticed the others dozing off to sleep as if nothing had happened, or simply continued to do what they were doing. It looked around to see if anyone else was doing anything different. Again, it tried to talk to itself, saying, "Maybe I shouldn't try anything new or different. This might be my fate and where I am born to be. Or, maybe I am going crazy!"

For an eagle, flying is not anything extraordinary. It is just doing what it was born to do. It's just the normal thing. Flying is the most ordinary thing an eagle could do. It was created for it. To do what it was born or created to do. What this eagle lacked was self-awareness. All it takes for that eagle to do what others thought was impossible or extraordinary, was self-awareness.

This book is not about doing something great or extraordinary. This is merely an inspiration for you to discover your true self, and to live what you were born to be. This is my sole motive.

It doesn't take or require anything special from you to do this. All it takes is to realize who you are, your true self, apart from whatever *chicken coops* you were brought up in or conditioned by.

When that happens, we realize who we really are for the first time, and this is called self-awareness. That is the beginning of life in God's kingdom.

Repentance versus Denial

When God created the first human being, his identity was not based on any nationality, job, race, color, name, skill, economic status, religious or political affiliation. He was the father of the human race. That is where each of us need to return to, in order to have self-awareness. This is called *repentance*. This is what Jesus meant when He said, "Repent for the kingdom of heaven is here."

We are all in this process at the moment. The whole earth and the entire human species are going through this process, regardless of our religious or nationalistic views. Some are ahead of others. Many are still in denial.

Many are trying to *tweak* their 'chicken coops' in order to make them look better. Thus, we created religion, denominations, ministries, churches, built cathedrals; placing ourselves under enormous burdens and fakeness. As a result, we are not only unable to *fly,* but many can barely even *crawl*.

To *repent* simply means to go back to where you came from, to return to the state you were created, to your original state, purpose, and intent.

For that eagle, to repent, doesn't mean feeling sorry for what it did for being raised in a chicken coop. It doesn't mean going to a religious place next Sunday morning and doing some rituals, singing some songs, or even waiting to go to heaven.

To that eagle, *repent* simply means to return to its original state, and do what it was created to do. It involves emptying itself from all knowledge, programming, and training it received from the chicken coop that caused it to think and function like a chicken—the false self and fake identity it received while growing up in a chicken coop.

The programming that robbed of its true identity and purpose, caused it to live this fake self, pretending to be a chicken, when it was not.

How do we know whether that eagle truly repented?

We know it repented, only if it does what it was born to do—which is to fly. No amount of religious duties, rituals, crying, feeling bad for itself for what it did or should have done will compensate or substitute for true repentance. If all those religious activities didn't lead that eagle to do what it was born to do, then all these accomplished was to add more fakeness to its already existing psychosis[2].

---

[2] Refers to a psychotic disturbance involving delusions, hallucinations, or disorganized speech or behavior; often occurring in reaction to a stressor - psychology-lexicon.com/

The same applies to us. We will know we truly repented when we realize *who* we are, and go back and start doing what God created us to do. Everything else we make and do doesn't matter how pious it may make us look, is a waste of time and life.

Repent means to go back to the beginning, and start all over again. The same applies to the Born Again experience. The purpose of being Born Again is to have a new beginning, a second birth.

We associate both repentance and the Born Again experience with stopping some bad habits that we call sins, changing religion or denominations. However, it really means stopping everything we were doing, by deleting every wrong belief system we were taught, and returning to the very *beginning*, as little children.

Then, from there, starting to learn what real life is supposed to be from God's perspective. As a result, any bad habits or sins we had, will fall off us. Anything that is not part of our true self and identity will be removed.

For this eagle:

> Merely stopping the flapping of its wings because this made the other chickens uncomfortable, or because they don't like it, is not repentance, or being nice. In fact, true repentance is flapping its wings until it flies—doing what it was born to do.

True Repentance

Now, the question is, how many of us are living truly repentant lives?

Many of us pride ourselves, saying, "I was Born Again when I was just four years old, or I received Jesus when I was just three years old. Or, I have been serving my church or ministry for so long—never missed a Sunday morning ritual.

That is not repentance. Nobody mentioned such *crazy* things anywhere in the Bible. The moment we start doing what we were created to do, that's when we can boldly say we have truly repented or Born Again—started life all over again for the right reason.

This is why Jesus said "many" would come that day and tell Him, "Lord in your name we cast out devils, and did many wonders and prophesied in Your name." Why was Jesus not impressed by any of those "great things" these people did for Him? They were involved in great ministries, and built mega-churches. These were not ordinary believers. These were gifted and famous people who did amazing things in the name of Jesus and for the Lord. They called Him "Lord."

None of those mighty works or ministries impressed Jesus. Why?

That was not what He created them to do. He did not authorize them to do any of those things. They were self-made, self-appointed or self-called ministers who lacked self-awareness. They did not take the time to stop and think for a moment why they were doing what they were doing, and who they really were. If this is the story of these gifted people, imagine the condition of the believers who followed them.

Jesus called them people who did lawlessness; or, in present day language, who are doing something illegal or doing something that is unauthorized.

Now the question is, why are you doing what you are doing with your life?

What are you doing with your life?

Can you answer this with radical honesty? Are you living from your authentic self or fake self? Are you living to fulfill your purpose, or trying to survive?

Principles of Self Governance

_____
_____
_____

Can you define yourself and your identity apart from your nationality, profession, race, religion, denomination, gender, skill, name or anything that was put on you after you were born?

_____
_____
_____
_____

You and your identity existed before you were born into the natural realm. When you realize this, you become self-aware of who you are for the first time, and that will lead you into self-discovery.

When we are self-aware, we are no longer doing something to become someone, but instead, we will start doing what we were born to do because we are already someone. When we are self-aware we will not be doing things to make others happy or for their acceptance, or to feel we fit in.

When we are self-aware we won't be living in survival mode, but will be fulfilling our purpose or destiny. We will be doing things and living life for the right reason for the first time. This is what we are going to discuss in the next chapter, called *self-discovery*.

Back to our eagle-saga:

> That eagle couldn't stop flapping its wings. Every time it saw another eagle in the air, this default response took over its entire being. The more it did it, the more it felt natural.

Chapter 1 | Self-Awareness

One day it flapped a little harder and longer; and to its amazement, it felt lifted off the ground. It could not believe what was happening. He was off the ground and all the chickens began to run in different directions—scared for their lives.

The mother hen shouted and screamed, saying to the eagle that it is so prideful and arrogant because it is doing something it was told not to do—doing something nobody in that chicken's family line had ever done before. The mother labeled that eagle disobedient and rebellious.

That eagle flew with ease outside the chicken coup and up into the air and into the unknown. It felt so natural.

Fulfilling our purpose is supposed to be natural. Meanwhile, back in the coop:

All the chickens looked on with amazement.

Everything this eagle thought impossible, was happening. It couldn't believe that what had kept it in the chicken coop for that long was its mind-set, or the way it had been thinking. That way of thinking was taught to it, so, it wasn't its fault.

A hen was not made to raise or teach eagles how to live or fly. A hen was made to raise other chickens.

Everything that was made, has a unique purpose; and was made to reproduce its own kind. We were created in the image and likeness of God, or we are the offsprings of God Almighty. We are supposed to reproduce the God-kind. We are supposed to function like God. What God is in heaven, we are supposed to be on the earth.

Since this eagle experienced what it thought was impossible, it couldn't go back to that chicken coop anymore. Not going back to the 'chicken coop' doesn't mean you don't *care* or you don't *love* those 'chickens' anymore.

Principles of Self Governance

Not going back to where you used to be is not pride, arrogance, or selfishness. It is being real and authentic. You can't go back because you have self-awareness, and that you were created to do something different.

> That single flight gave that eagle a different perspective about life and about chicken coops. It couldn't go back because it wasn't the same ever again.

Many of us are bound by the rules and regulations imposed by various *chicken coops* we grew up in. That causes us to live this fake self.

They created this boundary or ceiling that is invincible, but they are more than real. These limitations act as our 'master; and give rise to our theology; which in turn creates our reality. Then we ascribe 'divinity' to those rules and rituals, and believe these were imposed by or came from 'God'—when God was not responsible for anything that was happening in the first place.

Many people think the only thing God enjoys doing is imposing rules and rituals on human beings, and then punishing them if they don't keep them. Many destinies are robbed by these so-called 'masters.' People are imprisoned in these religious cages or prisons, and then their 'God factor' has a crippling effect on them, instead of being an empowering force.

Doing something different than what was taught in the 'chicken coop' will feel like going against the norm or even against God's rules or commandments. Especially if those rules were reinforced by any religion or by some Bible verses taken out of context, like built on the letter of the law of the Old Covenant. Fear will talk them out of moving forward—which prevents most people from coming to a place of self-awareness.

Once you reach that place of self-awareness, you will realize you were not made for rules and regulations; but these were made for you. We were not made for the Sabbath, but the Sabbath was made for us. Selah!

CHAPTER 1 | SELF-AWARENESS

Reflection and Action

Before we go any further, take a few *selah* moments for some self-assessment. Reflect on the foundations your life has been built upon, particularly those that may not align with God's truth. Use the following questions to explore these areas deeply, journal honestly, and take bold steps toward living from your true identity and purpose:

Radical honesty with yourself

1. Have you lived your life in radical honesty with yourself? Yes ☐   No ☐   *(If not, how?)*

_____

_____

_____

_____

2. Are you ready to answer the fundamental questions: *Who am I? Where did I come from? Why am I here?* Yes ☐   No ☐

3. Why are you doing what you're doing with your life?

_____

_____

_____

_____

Conformity versus authenticity

1. Did you begin anew when you were Born Again, or just carried everything over?

Principles of Self Governance

_____

_____

_____

_____

2. Have you conformed to a certain way of being just to blend in, avoid conflict, or keep others comfortable? Yes ☐   No ☐

3. Have you kept your *wings from flapping* so you wouldn't disturb the other *chickens*? Yes ☐   No ☐

4. What did you try to do in your life to build an identity?

_____

_____

_____

_____

Your foundation & formation

1. Was your life built on unconditional acceptance and love, or performance, and pressure?

_____

_____

_____

_____

2. Were you raised to fulfill your purpose, or to simply survive?

3. What was the primary "chicken coop" you were brought up in, and how has it shaped your sense of identity and self-worth?

Self-image & false Identity

1. Do you see yourself based on your true identity, or through masks and false narratives described by others and your culture?

2. Have you been living from a false identity without realizing it? Yes ☐ No ☐

3. What's your current identity based on, and who gave you that identity?

Principles of Self Governance

_____

_____

_____

4. What factors (culture, religion, family, trauma, education, etc.) shaped your current self-image?

_____

_____

_____

5. What needs to be surrendered in order to return to your authentic self?

_____

_____

_____

Fear & resistance

1. What fears are holding you back from leaving the fake self and false identity? (fear, rejection, failure, being misunderstood…)

_____

_____

_____

2. What's keeping you from doing what you were born to do?

Repentance & renewal

1. Based on what you've read, where are you in the process of true repentance and the Born Again experience?

2. When did you last ask yourself whether you're living from your authentic self or just surviving?

3. What do you need to do in order to go back to the beginning, and start doing what God created you to do?

To know more about your true identity, birthright, and inheritance in God's kingdom please read *God's Original Design book.*

CHAPTER 2

What is Self-Awareness?

Real life begins when we reach the point of self-awareness

Until then, we will be living someone else's definition of what life is all about, or by the dictates of fear and selfishness. Unfortunately, most people won't even arrive at self-awareness in this life. Imagine the loss this world incurs because of that. This is the reason why the world we live in is the way it is currently.

Imagine you entrust the whole world to people who are not aware of who they are. Who are living a fake self and in their false identities. They will start fighting each other. Since they don't know who they are, they won't know the purpose of creation. They will squander, lie, steal, pollute, and mismanage the resources. And instead of doing what God created them to do, they will start oppressing and enslaving one another.

Self-awareness is the ability to identify your true and authentic self without being influenced by the culture, religion, race, nationality, politics, money, or any other external forces or status.

If we examine all the problems we face in our lives and in the world around us, we will come to realize that these all stem from one of those external forces or ingredients I mentioned above. Politics, race, religion, money, status, power, you name it, all of them we fight and argue about—are things that don't truly matter. These were imposed on us to divide us and to cause us to fight each other.

What really matters is, do we know *who* we are, *where* we come from, and *why* are we here?

Can you identify some of the problems your community or nation is facing at the moment, and their root causes?

_____

_____

_____

The reason we fight and argue about all those things is because we lack *self-awareness*. The root of all problems we face in our world today is because we are living from a fake self that was imposed on us.

Self-awareness has a variety of dimensions because our *self* is made of many ingredients. The following, are just some of them:

Spiritual Awareness

You and I are spirit-beings sent from a kingdom called heaven to accomplish a mission on the earth. In order to make us legitimate entities on the earth, we are required to have a physical body. Any spirit without a physical body is illegal on the earth.

To be able to communicate between our spirit and body, we have a soul or mind. Our mind is a receiver and a processor which takes what is in our spirit, the world around us, and from the imaginary world, our experience; and decodes these into images and languages that we can understand, perceive or know. We are not merely our mind or body. We are spirits who have a mind and live in a body.

Primary Awareness

Primary awareness is *spiritual awareness.* You need to know that you are a spirit-being—not merely a body with feelings walking around and doing life.

There is a spiritual dimension to life, and many people are being awakened to it now, more than ever. More and more people are beginning to realize that there is a spirit-world and what is happening in their lives could be influenced by some evil spirits or some call it negative energy. They are beginning to understand and are trying to tap into a dimension that is beyond their natural sight and feelings. Some call this *universe* or *higher self* or *consciousness.*

You need to know that some things that are happening to you are spiritual in nature. And the spirit world is divided into two—God's world and the demonic world. There are spirit-beings that are assigned to help you, that are from God; and also those assigned to destroy you, from the devil or Satan.

Are you aware of your spirit in spite of or without any religious rituals, habits, music or church attendance?

Most people become a puppet of their religious orientation. They then try to fit God into the same religious box. Only when they "do" certain religious rituals do they become aware of their spirit. This is immature, short-sighted, and extremely dangerous. This is one of the dangers of being part of any religion.

We should be aware of our spirit and God just like we are aware of our soul and body.

The reason we are not normally aware of our spirit, is because we have not spent any time or effort to develop or grow our spirit as much as we did with our body and mind. Just like we feel weak physically if we don't feed and take care of our body, if we don't train our spirit, we will not be aware of it.

Just like our body needs food and our mind needs to be educated, our spirit needs to be developed with *proper* food. Our body needs natural food, our mind needs intellectual food, and our spirit needs spiritual food. Our spirit needs to be connected to its Creator or Source—which is God. We relate to Him as our Father. *Father* simply means source.

Why does God want us to relate with Him as our Father? Everyone is looking for a father or a father figure. This is why people are attracted to coaches, mentors, and some get attached to gurus and other religious figures. The reason we are longing for a father figure is because we feel they have the answers that we need for our lives. Those gurus and religious figures don't have answers because they are fake in themselves. They themselves are looking for answers.

Some end up with the wrong person, gender, group or gangs searching for this father figure. The absence of mature fathers in families and communities, together with father-related wounds or issues, is the root of most of the social problems we have in our society today.

We will find the real source and the true meaning of our life only when we discover the source of our spirit—our heavenly Father. This is why God wants to relate with us as a Father. However, the abandonment, rejection, and abuse people experienced from fathers, religious, or authority figures, have created a wrong perception of God; causing people to run away from God, and wanting nothing to do with Him.

In order to correct this distorted perception of God, and to heal the wounds and abuses we experienced from fathers, or authority figures, we have prepared an excellent tool. *What Happened to God* **book. Please see the next page for more information.**

Chapter 2 | What is Self-Awareness?

Reflection and Action

1. Beyond your body, thoughts, emotions, culture, and religious background, who are you? What remains when you strip away everything you've been told you are?

   _____

   _____

   _____

2. Are you living with the daily awareness that you are a spirit-being sent from heaven on assignment, or have you become spiritually passive?

   _____

   _____

   _____

3. Have you tried to fit God into a box—whether shaped by religion, culture, fear, or your own experiences—instead of building a living relationship with Him as your Father? How has that limited your spiritual growth and understanding?

   _____

   _____

   _____

4. In what ways have you neglected or contributed to the development of your spirit compared to the care you give to your body or mind?

   _____

CHAPTER 2 | WHAT IS SELF-AWARENESS?

5. What would it look like to prioritize spiritual nourishment in your daily life?

_____
_____
_____

6. Are you aware that behind some of the circumstances, thoughts, or battles you face, there's a spiritual dimension—one which involves both God's Kingdom and the demonic realm? Do you recognize what's natural and what's spiritual, and whose voice is influencing you?

_____
_____
_____

7. Do you recognize the voice of God's Spirit in your life? What distracts you from hearing Him clearly and walking by His direction?

_____
_____
_____

In order to understand more and to dive deep into discovering God as our Father, and to understand our true identity as sons and daughters, we have prepared an excellent resource for you. *Relationship with the Father* **Workshop. This is a one of a kind manual tailored to fit your level, irrespective of whether you are a new believer or a seasoned one.**

Relationship with the Father
– WORKSHOP –

Why do we long for a **father figure**? Perhaps, deep down, we're searching for the **Father**.

KINGDOM DELIVERANCE
— WORKSHOP —
Live Your Destiny

RELATIONSHIP WITH THE FATHER

- We will learn why God wants us **to know Him as Father**, not just as Creator.
- How **parental wounds** influence our decisions, relationships, and spirituality.
- How to find **identity**, **security**, and **purpose** in an intimate relationship with your Heavenly Father.

RETURN TO THE FATHER

Your soul yearns for identity, love, and security. Many seek answers in human figures, but only the Heavenly Father can fill that void.
This workshop will help you restore that vital relationship with God.
If you long for this, then this resource is for you.

ORDER NOW
WWW.TREEOF-LIFE.COM

CHAPTER 2 | WHAT IS SELF-AWARENESS?

To know more about our spirit and what is happening in the spirit-world, we have an excellent resource for you. *Spiritual Healing* Workshop. This manual will help you identify the source of the battles you are facing, the blockage or the problem you are finding hard to identify or diagnose. This manual will open your eyes to the spiritual world and give you the keys to walk in victory.

Emotional Awareness

If you have been struggling with certain emotions for a period of time, then it is time to find out the root from where those emotions are coming from. What you are feeling is only a symptom. The real cause or root of that emotion will be obscured. It will take some digging to locate its root.

For example, if you feel that you are not good enough or performing to feel worthy or to be accepted, those emotions or actions are only symptoms. The root cause of those emotions and actions exist in a lack of self-love. You don't like or love yourself because you believe a lie about yourself.

The reason you don't love yourself is because you don't feel that you are worthy to be loved. The reason you feel you are not worthy is because you have not yet experienced the unconditional love of God for your life.

The reason you don't experience the unconditional love of God is because you did not receive unconditional love from your parents while growing up, particularly from your father. Some incidents may have occurred which caused you to believe that lie. That is the root. Until you deal with it and rectify this issue, those feelings and actions will not change.

One of the keys to being happy and grateful is to be aware and know what is happening in your emotional life. Know for sure that you are not what you feel. Our emotions lie to us all the time.

Most people deal with the symptoms and they try to medicate or soothe what they feel with some (bad) habits like drugs, alcohol, porn, or even the media. This is like putting a bandaid on a tumor. It is a temporary but deadly fix.

For example, if you don't feel accepted or are feeling rejected, then you may become a perfectionist, a workaholic, or a people-pleaser. Perfectionism, workaholism, and people-pleasing are only symptoms.

Chapter 2 | What is Self-Awareness?

Your life will be all about performance, you will be trying to "buy" love and acceptance from others by trying to please them. If you don't feel loved by God, you could end up looking for love in the wrong places or from the wrong people.

What is the image or voice that you keep seeing or replaying in the back of your mind or your subconscious mind?

Whether it is negative or positive, that is your current ceiling, reality, or boundary in the spirit-world. The same principle applies to every other area or aspect of your life. For example, what you keep replaying in your subconscious mind about your future, finances, or any other areas of your life is your ceiling; and these have the potential to keep you bound to that level.

If you are struggling with rejection, fear, anxiety, addiction, low self-esteem, insecurity, underperformance, workaholism, stress, depression, lack of money, over- or underweight issues; these are all only symptoms. The root issue may be something that happened to you, or which you went through when you were a child that created your subsequent belief system. You became a prisoner of those belief systems. You need to be set free from this prison.

Every emotion we feel has a source and a root. Emotion is simply energy in motion. Whether these are negative or positive ones, they cause a reciprocal effect in our body and mind. They reproduce their own kind.

Reflection and Action

1. Which of the following core beliefs do you recognize in yourself?

   ☐ I am not good enough   ☐ I am powerless to change my situation

   ☐ I am unlovable   ☐ Something is wrong with me

Principles of Self Governance

☐ I am not worthy

☐ I always fail

☐ I don't matter

☐ I have to earn love and approval

2. Which of these negative thoughts do you find yourself thinking regularly?

☐ No one really cares about me.

☐ I'll never have enough, no matter what I do.

☐ Why try? I'll just fail again.

☐ I have to make everyone happy

☐ Others always do better than me.

☐ I can't do anything right.

☐ I'm a burden to others.

☐ I'm too damaged to be loved.

☐ I'll never change.

3. Which of these behaviors have you noticed in your life?

☐ I try to please everyone, even when it drains me

☐ I avoid difficult situations or people

☐ I work excessively in order to feel valuable

☐ I sabotage good opportunities or relationships

☐ I isolate myself when I feel overwhelmed

☐ I struggle to say "no" even when I want to

☐ I depend on substances or habits to numb my emotional pain

Chapter 2 | What is Self-Awareness?

☐ I jump from one thing to another without following-through

☐ I constantly seek approval or validation from others

4. Which of the following physical symptoms have you experienced regularly?

☐ Fatigue that seemingly doesn't go away with rest

☐ Headaches or migraines under stress

☐ Trouble sleeping (too much, or too little)

☐ Digestive issues with no medical cause

☐ Tension in your neck, shoulders, or jaw

☐ Sudden weight gain, or loss

☐ Shortness of breath, or tightness in my chest

☐ My heart racing when facing pressure

☐ Frequent colds, sweats, or a weakened immune system

5. Have you confused emotional pain with your identity, believing that how you feel is who you are? Yes ☐   No ☐

6. Are you ready to stop treating the symptoms and finally confront the root, no matter how deep or painful it is, so you can be free? Yes ☐   No ☐

It is impossible to add solutions to all the above-mentioned questions in this book. You may have answered *Yes* to many of the above questionnaires yet wondering what you should do now?

Don't worry or feel frustrated, we have prepared the tool you need. This *Emotional Healing* Workshop manual will help you deal with all of the above-mentioned emotions, their roots, and more.

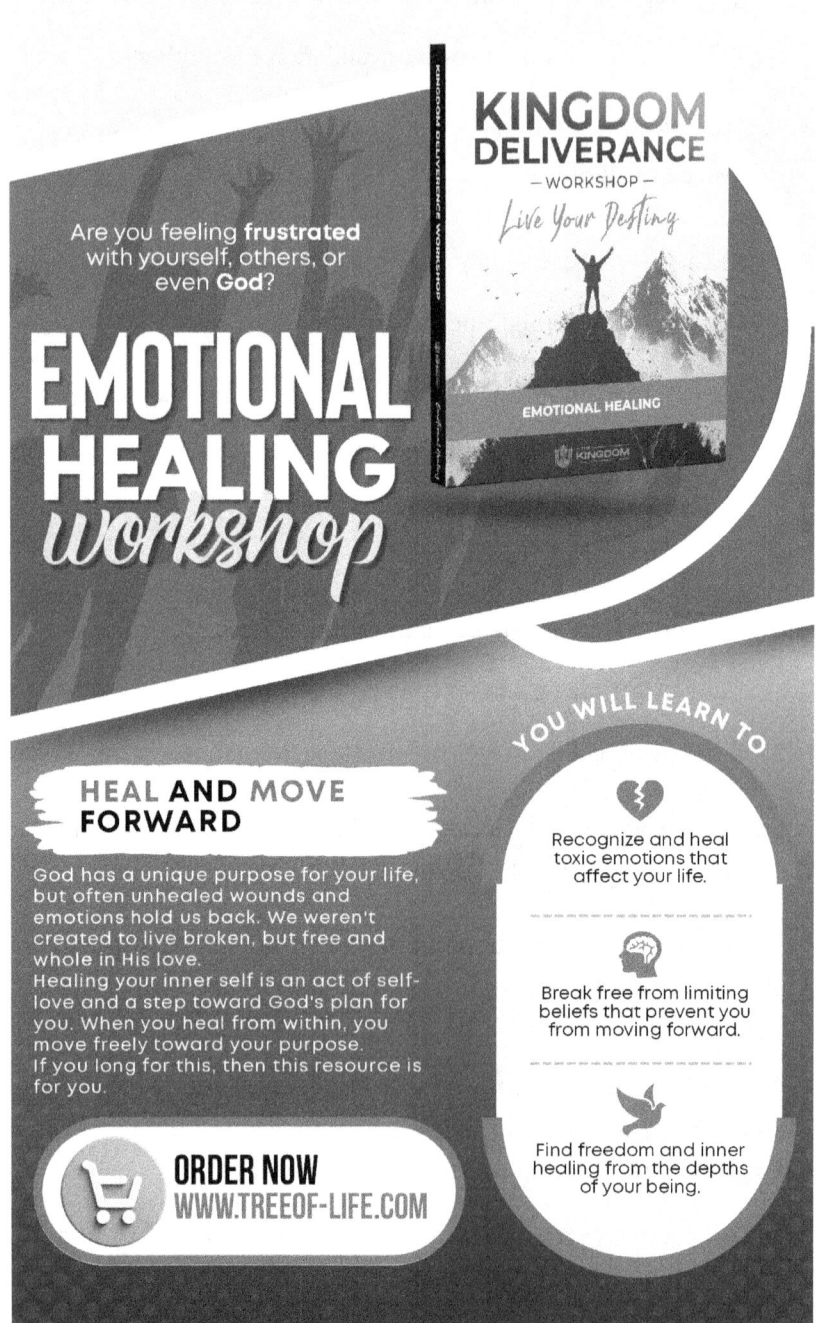

Physical Awareness

Do you know what is happening inside your body? Are you aware of it? Our body is designed in a way that it communicates in unique ways what is happening inside it.

Again what you feel or see on the surface might only be a symptom. Whether it is emotional or physical, always keep in mind not to treat the symptoms; but rather, identify and deal with the cause or the root as early as possible, not just the fruit.

It is like the light or sign that flashes on the dashboard of a car. Those lights or icons are only a warning sign that indicates that there is something which needs attention within that car. The solution is not replacing or getting rid of the dashboard or the light. It won't solve the issue.

Many people make the mistake of postponing to deal with the issues that they feel in their mind and body, and so wait until the last minute or until something serious happens. Please don't wait till it is too late. Address and take care of these NOW.

Take care of your spirit, soul, and body equally. Don't ignore one or be partial. All three are equally important. One won't work properly without the other. If one breaks down or dysfunctions, it will affect the other two areas as well.

Are you aware of the effect of the food you eat, air you breathe, and what you drink to your body and brain? These things won't show up in a day or two. It takes years, as our body is built to last and to tolerate a lot of abuse and toxins. However, habits are hard to change, so it is important to build healthy habits from the start. Prevention is better than cure.

Habit and Word Awareness

Under physical awareness comes **habit awareness**. Once we form certain habits and form a lifestyle based on those habits, life becomes predictable.

We don't need a prophet to come and tell us what is going to happen in our life and where we are going to end up. Those habits, whether good or bad, can predict our future for the most part.

Words awareness is another important one. Are we aware of the words we speak on a regular basis? Everything visible and invisible was created by words, thoughts, or ideas.

God "spoke" everything into existence. In essence, thoughts and ideas are words. The world we see around us was created by our words, thoughts, ideas, and actions collectively.

It is meaningless to blame anyone else. If we need to change the world, then we need to start with changing *how* and *what* we think and speak.

The whole of creation is affected and influenced by our words. We shouldn't underestimate the power of our words. We can bless or curse. We can speak either life or death.

Words are seeds. Every seed is designed to reproduce its own kind. Sooner or later, we will experience the fruit of those words. Everything I am experiencing in my life right now are the result of the words I spoke decades ago. This is one of the most important principles the Lord ever taught me since I was seventeen years old.

Reflection and Action

1. Are there recurring physical symptoms that you've ignored and haven't truly addressed? Yes ☐   No ☐ *(If Yes, Which ones?)*

_____
_____
_____
_____

Chapter 2 | What is Self-Awareness?

2. Are you postponing care for your body, thinking "I'll deal with it later"? What would it take for you to prioritize proper prevention today?

_____

_____

_____

3. What physical habits are you building today that will shape your health 5, 10, or 20 years from now?

_____

_____

_____

Your body is the temple of God—the only temple that is authorized by God on the earth. It is important to take excellent care of it. To assist you with taking the best care of your body and its needs, we have prepared the best tool. The *Physical Health Workshop*. Order your copy today. Please see next page for more details.

Chapter 2 | What is Self-Awareness?

Habits Awareness

"You will reap what you sow." – Galatians 6:7

Psychology confirms that almost 50% of our actions each day are habits, not decisions[3].

Habits are supposed to be aligned with your values and goals so they serve you instead of enslaving you.

Check whether each habit below applies to your life, and evaluate whether it is life-giving or life-draining in your current season:

Habit	**Do I Do This? (Yes/No)**	**Life-Giving**	**Life-Draining**
I consume fast food, sugar, or caffeine excessively	☐ Yes ☐ No	☐	☐
I sleep 7–8 hours consistently	☐ Yes ☐ No	☐	☐
I move my body regularly (walking, stretching, exercising)	☐ Yes ☐ No	☐	☐
I rest consciously	☐ Yes ☐ No	☐	☐
I depend on substances (alcohol, nicotine, or medication) to cope with stress or moods	☐ Yes ☐ No	☐	☐

---

3 Duke University study by Dr. Wendy Wood published in Wood, Quinn, & Kashy (2002). *"Habits in Everyday Life: Thought, Emotion, and Action."* Journal of Personality and Social Psychology, 83(6), 1281–1297.

What small but intentional step will you take this week to align with the life you were created to live? *This week, I will:* _____

_____

_____

Words Awareness

If my words are seeds, what kind of "harvest" am I beginning to see in my life as a result of the words I have consistently spoken about myself, others, or my future?

_____

_____

_____

_____

Financial Awareness

Most people get stuck in either the rat race or the mundane nature of life and develop certain unhealthy habits along the way. These bad habits can be emotional, physical or financial.

Your financial life or condition is only a reflection, result, or fruit. Financial conditions or poverty are only symptoms. Where you are financially at the moment, is a direct result of your self-awareness and financial discipline, or the lack of it.

Most people blame others, the economy of their country, and family for their financial condition. They do this because they lack financial-awareness. Your current financial status is only a reflection of the well-being and productivity of your soul, spirit, and body.

Chapter 2 | What is Self-Awareness?

You may be told that you need to go to school to get an education; and, you need an education to find a good job; and, you need a nice job to make some money; and, you need money to live and pay for things. This is the conditioning most of us grew up with. But that is a big lie.

We were living someone else's definition of life. Like I said earlier, real life only starts with self-awareness. Once you apply the steps mentioned in this book, it's just a matter of time, it will change your financial status.

Many people lack the discipline and knowledge of proper money management because their needs are always more than the money they make. Rather, they *believe* that their needs are more than the money they have or make.

One of the reasons why they feel like that, is they are trying to live someone else's definition of life which came from a fake self, or comparing themselves with others, or trying to live a status quo which they can't afford to live.

Financial awareness is knowing how much money is coming to you at the moment, and planning a lifestyle that you can afford; and then saving some, and making plans to move up or to go to the next level. This is financial awareness.

If you have been living above your income for a long time, your expenditure is more than your income. If you keep blaming others for your problem, then the problem is not money or others; the real problem is lack of financial awareness. This could be rooted in some emotional wounds you carry from childhood which you are trying to medicate by overspending; or by being lazy; or it could be lack of financial discipline or the lack of money management skills.

When it comes to money, you cannot put the cart before the horse. I mean, you cannot pretend to live a lifestyle that you cannot afford. If you do, you won't be able to live and sleep in peace. You will always be under a lot of pressure and stress. Eventually your mind and body will feel the effect of all that stress and pressure.

But if you live a lifestyle that you can afford, living below your means, knowing it is temporary, saving, and putting the necessary tools and systems in place to multiply the money you have, and learning about money and how it works; then you will be able to take full advantage of it. If you do this you will not remain poor or broke for very long.

Reflection and Action

Are you living below your means so you can save, give, and invest in what truly matters? ☐ Yes ☐ No (If no, please elaborate)

_____

_____

_____

_____

How often do your financial decisions come from a place of worry instead of trust in God's provision?

_____

_____

_____

_____

Are you educating yourself on how to manage and grow the resources God has entrusted to you (like budgeting, debt reduction, investments)?

_____

Chapter 2 | What is Self-Awareness?

_____

_____

_____

Are you willing to change your habits, learn new skills, and surrender your finances to God's governance?

_____

_____

_____

In what ways are you using your money to build God's Kingdom rather than just your own comfort or status?

_____

_____

_____

Your current financial condition is only a reflection of the state and productivity of your soul, spirit, and body. You can change this by learning the right skills and taking proper action.

The freer you become emotionally and spiritually, the more your financial situation will also change for the better. To learn more about financial awareness, please see the details below for how you can order the *Finance—Learning to live in the Kingdom Economy Workshop* resource. Please see the next page for more details

Social Awareness

Are you aware of the people who are around you and within your social circle or community? Do you genuinely care about them? Are you aware that what you do with your life and how you live affects others, in one way or another?

We are social beings. We are connected to one another in more ways than we are aware. We need to be our brothers' keeper.

When was the last time you reached out to someone and showed them that you care? It could be a stranger, family member, or someone that you know. Each one of us is an important piece of the puzzle of life. The community we live in is expecting our contribution. The whole of creation is waiting for us.

People everywhere are becoming more exclusively individualistic socially. They don't genuinely care about others. It is because they lack social awareness and skills. In some cultures it is possible to live in a neighborhood and not know who is living next door. They lack social awareness.

When the social foundations of family, community, and connections are broken, social ills manifest themselves in society. Drug problems, prostitution, stealing, sex- and human trafficking, and corruption are just some of these.

According to Jesus, our neighbor is whosoever is in need of help. We shouldn't close our eyes and hearts from reaching out because the color or the race of the person is different from ourselves.

Despite there being more people alive on the earth today than at any other time, loneliness is the number one issue people face everywhere. Feeling isolated, rejected, or bullied are major social problems of our day.

Reflection and Action

When was the last time you intentionally reached out to someone in need, even when it was inconvenient or uncomfortable for you?

_____

_____

_____

Are you living as if your life belongs only to you, or do you see yourself as part of something bigger; a family, a community, a purpose God has placed you in?

_____

_____

_____

What might be the deeper reasons behind your lack of empathy or disconnection from the needs of others in your life?

_____

_____

_____

Environmental Awareness

Are we aware of the environment around us that we live in? Do we know how our environment is affected by the way we live and what we use?

Chapter 2 | What is Self-Awareness?

We are responsible to take care of the environment, protect, and conserve it. Our environment is what a womb is to a baby. It is *that* important. Most people take it for granted, and are not aware of what is happening around them and how the environment is impacted by the way they live and what they do.

There is so much talk and political activity about taking care of or fixing the environment. Billions of dollars are spent on it. But if each individual accepts the responsibility for taking care of the environment and the surroundings they live in, then there is no need for any political involvement. We need to teach environmental awareness to our children while they are still very young.

Even big corporations are established and run by individuals. If they are responsible individuals then they wouldn't do anything to harm their environment.

In some places the environment has become unlivable. The quality of the air, water and the soil can no longer sustain human beings. It is going to take some expertise and resources to clean up the mess we created.

Reflection and Action

Do you believe your small actions can make a real difference, or have you fallen into the mindset that what you do is too insignificant to impact large problems?

_____

_____

_____

_____

_____

Review each action and mark whether it is something you currently do or not.

Practical Action	Yes	No
I turn off lights and unplug devices when not in use	[ ]	[ ]
I reduce car use by walking, biking, carpooling, or using public transportation	[ ]	[ ]
I recycle properly and separate waste as required	[ ]	[ ]
I use water wisely and avoid wasting it at home	[ ]	[ ]
I teach my children about the importance of caring for the environment	[ ]	[ ]

Are you willing to take individual action to help improve an environmental issue in your area? ☐ Yes, I commit to take action.

If yes, what specific action will you take?

_____

_____

_____

_____

Once we reach self-awareness, we will need to make some changes. We can't or won't be able to live the way we used to. If we try to live the way we used to and do the same old thing, then we will be deceiving ourselves. Though it might take some time, effort and overcoming fears to make the necessary changes, it will be worth it.

Don't be in a hurry or hasten to make the changes. Know that it took you many years to reach where you are; and so, change won't happen in a day or two. Be patient with yourself and with others around you. Let this revelation sink in and take root.

Then, when the right time comes you will know it is time to leave your *chicken coop*.

CHAPTER 3

Leaving Your *Chicken Coop*

Have you ever wished there was at least one person who would truly understand you?

What would you do with your life if fear was not present?

The reason we ask these questions is because we are not living our true self yet, as we have not yet reached self-awareness. We are living in self-rejection or denial.

Moses—'Prince of Egypt'

Moses was one of the most influential persons who ever lived on the earth. However, his life did not start out all glorious. He grew up without his natural parents. I can imagine him struggling with the feelings of abandonment, rejection, and insecurity that came from his fatherless wounds.

Historians say his stuttering started as a result of his parents choking his throat trying to quiet or stop him from crying when he was a baby. He was born into fear with a death sentence looming over his head. He was hidden from the authorities for his first three months in order to escape the consequences of the dire decree of the king that stated all male children had to be put to death.

When Moses couldn't be hidden any longer, his mother put him in a basket and sent him away down the Nile River. He was eventually found by the daughter of the Pharaoh, who took him into the palace where she adopted and brought him up as her son.

For Moses his *chicken coop* was not a poverty-stricken neighborhood of the most populated city, but it was the palace of the most powerful and richest kingdom at that time. He was born a slave, but was taken and adopted by the ruling family as one of their heirs.

Growing up in the palace as a prince, he had everything any child could ever dream of. Moses had servants at his bidding, and lavish gardens in his backyard. He may even have had a lion cub as his pet. His position and his title in the royal family were all lined up. He did not have to worry about anything. All he had to do was just to grow up and function in the role that was designated and waiting for him.

There was only one problem though. Everything he was living and experiencing were not based in truth, it was all based on lies and a fake self and false identity that were put on him.

In reality, he was not the prince of Egypt by any means. But everyone else around him, his name, his title, his dress code, the culture he was growing up in, what people thought of and called him, his government-issued ID—all said he was the prince of Egypt. In reality, he was none of those things. What an irony of fate!

Moses was not just any person or merely the tragic subject of an isolated story. Moses represents each one of us. We are all in the same boat as Moses was. When we hear his story, we feel sympathy for what happened to him. Or, some may feel jealous, because who does not want to have all that he had in the palace. Who wouldn't want to grow up as a

Chapter 3 | Leaving Your Chicken Coop

royal prince? That would be the dream life of many. They believe luxury and material wealth would make them happy and fulfilled. Ask Moses.

The reality is, what happened to Moses, happened to each one of us. We may not have been adopted by some royal family and had the opportunity to grow up in a palace. That depends on our destiny.

The reason we can't identify with Moses, is because we have not reached self-awareness yet. We are all sent by heaven to earth to accomplish an assignment for the King of heaven. We have a limited amount of time to do it.

Most people are not free to do what they were born to do. They are crying out in silence for help, but no one hears their cry. Some people have no more tears left to cry. They have been taken captive by *Egypt;* but nevertheless, many of them have the necessities and conveniences they need for life, so they are not destitute.

What they are all missing in fact, is *purpose* and *fulfillment.* Convenience without purpose is frustration and unfulfillment. Luxury without a vision to fulfill, is wastefulness. Life without a mission and the freedom to do what you were born to do, is slavery.

Egypt represents two things. First of all, it represents a country in Northern Africa. Second it represents a system and lifestyle that is deeply rooted in religion, witchcraft, and occultism. This is the reason Egypt is mentioned in the Bible from Genesis to Revelation.

Most of us are affected by religion in one way or another. We have spent many years treading the same waters, only to realize we haven't reached very far with our lives.

Write your experience in religion and the effect of it on your life

_____

_____

Principles of Self Governance

When we were born, we were taken captive; and a fake self and a false identity were imposed on us. We became the property of some government. Then we spent the rest of our lives paying taxes to that government.

We pledged our allegiance to things that don't really matter. Then we spent the rest of our lives trying to protect what is fake and to make some money in order to take care and preserve that fake self. I call it the post-modern day glorified system of slavery. Whoever you are afraid of displeasing, becomes your 'slave master.'

They call us the "working class" or the "taxpayers." In reality we are the "slave class." For example, my income tax bracket is more than 20%. That means I have to pay the government more than twenty percent of everything I make. I don't have a choice over the matter. On top of that, I need to pay taxes on everything I buy—the food that I eat, clothes that I wear, even the toilet tissue—everything is taxed. The services I use, like phone, wifi, car, etc. all come with taxes; which means, when you go to work, more than half of your time and skills are spent making your government rich.

The balance of my income goes to some businesses, big corporations, or banks for the products and services I use; like housing, health insurance, interest, etc. Even 'God' required only ten-percent from the people. Then we pride ourselves saying we are living in a free society or even serving God.

This is the biggest scam ever to happen to humanity. This is why Jesus said, no one can serve two masters. Can you imagine Christians thinking they are serving God because they go to church for two hours on a Sunday and give a tip in the offering basket! Lord have mercy! We were created to love and serve God with all our heart, mind, and strength.

Chapter 3 | Leaving Your Chicken Coop

When we were born naturally, we were born into a kingdom. Whichever country you were born in, that country is ruled by the kingdom of darkness.

We were brought up by people who themselves had not reached self-awareness. They then imposed on us what they believed was true to them—like the hen did to that eagle.

When we were born, we were all born into a culture, religion, nationality, educational, and a political system. We inherited these as part of our lives. We accepted these and thought they were all part of normal life.

Most people won't recognize their true self or their assignment they were sent here for. They live and die without ever discovering their purpose and true identity.

One good thing about Moses was he began to face unusual crises in his life. Nothing he had or did brought any fulfillment to him. He felt like he was wasting his life, or something did not feel quite right inside him.

These circumstances led him on a deep search. He decided to go behind the scenes, and go deeper than his apparent reality. Instead of merely dealing with the symptoms, he decided to look for the root cause. One day he decided to take a long walk to the slave camp. Something unusual happened to him there which changed the course of his life:

> Now it came to pass in those days, when Moses was grown, that he went out to his brethren and looked at their burdens and he saw an Egyptian beating a Hebrew, one of his brethren.
>
> So he looked this way and that way, and when he saw no one, he killed the Egyptian and hid him in the sand.
>
> And when he went out the second day, behold, two Hebrew men were fighting, and he said to the one who did the wrong, "Why are you striking your companion?"

Then he said, "Who made you a prince and a judge over us? Do you intend to kill me as you killed the Egyptian?"
– Exodus 2:11-14 NKJV

This is very key, because most people waste their crises thinking these are just misfortunes, or they blame God, the devil, or others for it. They live in regret. Most people spend their entire lives dealing with the symptoms, and not finding any real root or cure for their problems.

Every crisis was allowed into our lives so that we would go on a deep search—to go deeper than what is apparent, and what we perceive and comprehend with our five senses; in order to discover something we never knew existed about ourselves. This is the purpose of crises.

Are you going through any crisis at the moment? Describe it.

_____

_____

_____

_____

Does that crisis cause you to go and search deeper? Write the results you found about life and yourself:

_____

_____

_____

_____

Moses' *chicken coop* was not a cheap one. It was the most luxurious and expensive one in monetary value. It was not easy for him to walk away from it all. But his deep search helped him discover some truths

Chapter 3 | Leaving Your Chicken Coop

about his life, which changed the course of his life. He now understood the reason behind all the dissatisfaction he was feeling—why he couldn't fit in, no matter how hard he tried.

His soul and heart wouldn't come into alignment with his surroundings and his relationships that were around him in the palace. The reason was, he was not supposed to be there.

Rather, he was sent there for two reasons—to see and observe the sufferings of his brethren—so that he could have an eyewitness experience of the maltreatment his people were facing on a daily basis. He also needed to know the mysterious Egyptian system that was deeply rooted in religion and occult, and how it operated; which was afflicting and enslaving his people, and was abusing and robbing them of their respective destinies.

Growing up in the palace gave him first-hand knowledge about the deeply religious and occultic practices of the ruling class or the government of Egypt. In our post-modern day, we call this the *deep state*. This is the reason some of us had the privilege of growing up in different religions, and under different forms of governments.

Looking on from the outside, people and nations thought and saw Egypt as the most powerful military and prosperous kingdom at that time. Inside, it was a whole different story. Only a few knew and understood what made Egypt that powerful and the foundations on which it was built. It was built on mammon, a system built on economy, religion (occult), and government.

The Israelites were God's people, but they were not free to serve God or to do what they were born to do. They were forced to serve another master for their survival. This is the story of most people and nations that exist today. We need another Moses and another exodus.

That was the purpose of his or our fake self; and the purpose of the eagle's 'chicken coop'—to know what life is *not*; to identify with people where they are at; to know what is happening behind the scenes to the rulers of darkness and the governments of this world.

Once we come out of our *chicken coop* we understand the difference between what is real and what is fake. Then we are ready to go back and deliver others, as Moses did.

Moses decided to confront his fake self and deny or reject it. This is the self-denial each of us need to go through. This is what Jesus was talking about.

Jesus—'the Carpenter'

Jesus had to do this as well. He was a Jewish carpenter and people identified Him with that skill. He did carpentry work because his stepfather, Joseph, did it. People called Him the "son of a carpenter."

He had to deny that false identity in order to step into the assignment He was born to do; by receiving His true identity and approval as a "beloved Son" from His real Father. This needs to happen to every single human being.

Paul the Apostle

The Apostle Paul had to go through this process. He denied his Jewish and educated self, and decided to carry the cross instead.

Can you recognize the day and moment when this event occurred in your life? Can you describe the incident?

_____
_____
_____
_____

I am not talking about someone mumbling some prayer and saying they received Jesus in order to go to heaven. Most do this to preserve their fake self, not to deny it. This is not how people in the Bible did it.

Paul was from the tribe of Benjamin, he was a prominent Pharisee who had been trained under Gamaliel. This is like someone saying they were born into some prominent family, and they graduated from some well-known university. But that was his fake self.

Leaving the *Pig Pen*

Many of us are familiar with the story of the prodigal son Jesus shared in the Gospel of Luke chapter 15. A certain father had two sons. The younger one came to the father and asked him for his inheritance. The father gave it to him and he sold everything, turning it into cash, and left his father's house for a far away country.

This son lacked self-awareness, and never went through the process of self-discovery to know *who* he was. That is the main reason he decided to run away from his father.

He thought life would be better off without his father, and so, he sought out a community where he could do whatever he wanted to do. While he was away, he wasted all his money and was abandoned by his riotous companions. He was hungry, and looked around for a job. All that he could find was a job feeding the swine. He ate the swine's food and slept in their pig pen.

That crisis brought him to a place of self-awareness. The Bible says, "he came to himself" (Luke 15:17). While in the pig pen he had a revelation of who he really was—where he came from, who his father was, and what he had at his father's house. Although he felt unworthy, he decided to return to his father's house; where his father received him gladly, and restored his sonship.

This needs to happen to each one of us. This story has nothing to do with going to church or heaven. We belong to our heavenly Father and each one of us decided to run away from him and take life into our own hands. We thought we could build a better life without Him. Then at some point we realized what we thought was better, was not really better. We ended up as slaves to another master, eating swine's food.

The Prodigal son did not stop at self-awareness. He went through each of the processes mentioned in this book. May the Lord help us to do the same.

To know more about the Prodigal son and why he decided to leave his father's house; and about his older brother, I have written about this extensively in *God's Original Design* book.

A New Beginning

When we are Born Again we are supposed to start life all over again. Everything we were until then is considered *old*. Our nationality, race, mistakes, sins, status, name, religious and political affiliation, etc. become part of that old fake self. It's a new beginning.

We cannot carry the old into the new. It is the beginning of doing what God created us to do. We receive a new name, a new nationality, new citizenship, true identity, new family, and a new mission. This is the purpose of being Born Again. It is not merely stopping some bad habits or just changing religion, and not to reserve a ticket to go to heaven after we die.

People wonder why we don't see God doing things like He did in the Bible days. In order for us to see what they saw, we need to do what they did. They were not all drunkards and drug users who heard the gospel and then received Jesus to go to heaven. They were normal people like most of us—doing something to make a living. At some point they came to a place of self-awareness and started life all over again.

The Three Thousand

Especially the 3000 people who became part of the *Ekklesia* in the book of Acts. They did not see any miracles that day, nor did they raise their hands to go to heaven or repeat any prayer after someone. They were not all poor people either. They were influential people who came from all over the world to Jerusalem to observe a feast.

What happened to them that day was that they changed kingdoms. They transitioned from one kingdom to another—from serving one king or lord, to serving another.

They did not merely stop some bad habits and start going to some religious buildings on a weekend. What happened to them was that their mission in life was changed. They left their *chicken coop*.

The Disciples

This is what the disciples did when they had an encounter with Jesus. They stopped doing whatever they were doing for making a living, and started doing something totally different. They started doing what they were born to do. This is called *self-discovery*.

Through their encounter with the Creator and by being Born Again, they came to a place of realization of the reason why they were sent to this earth for. They left whatever they were doing for their survival, and started doing what they were created for. This is called true repentance and this is called true salvation. This is why Jesus came and died for us. This must happen to each one of us.

Fleeing the 'Coop'

Some of our chicken coops may not be as glorious as Moses' and Paul's were. We may not have anything to boast about. The truth is, whether it is glorious or ordinary, are we able to identify our 'chicken coop' or are we still blindsided?

Many boast about their chicken coop. Instead of leaving it, some even try to *decorate* it with more performance, rituals, certificates, and titles. Some even go to the extent of paying penance for their sins. Apostle Paul called his chicken coop "dung." That is what you will find in every chicken coop, chicken poop. He had to leave everything behind in order to fulfill the calling on his life. May the Lord help each one of us to identify and leave our chicken coops.

In order to leave our chicken coop we need to overcome the fear of losing what we thought was secure, what gave us our false identity; and then step out into the unknown. Only God will be there to hold us together.

People tend to come up with all kinds of excuses for why they want to continue to live in their 'chicken coop.' They just don't want to admit it and get rid of their ego or pride which is built around *their* 'chicken coop.'

They don't want to give up their false or fake self and identity. They don't want to take up the cross and follow Jesus. Their motto is self-preservation. They make an idol of their fake self. The root of all these is fear and pride.

Can you identify your 'chicken coop'?

What would it take for you to leave it, and step into what you were born to do?

_____

_____

_____

_____

Only when we are self-aware of who we are and why we are here, are we in a position to help others. This is why governments and all Non Governmental Organizations (NGOs) are failing in their mission. Most of them are run by people who lack self-awareness.

Lessons from Moses' Example

Again, if we look at Moses' life we see this same pattern. He couldn't help his people until he reached the place of self-awareness, which led to self-discovery.

When we are self-aware we will be aware of who others are, where they are in life, and what they are going through. Until then, we will try to impose on others what we believe, our opinion, and our agenda which causes division, sectarianism, and rebellion.

Twice, Moses tried to solve social problems before he reached self-awareness and self-discovery; and both times these misfired.

Once, when he saw an Egyptian beating an Israelite, he became angry and took the situation into his own hands, killing the Egyptian. This is why people kill each other. They think they are doing it for the right reason, or doing it for their *god*. That crisis eventually caused Moses to leave Egypt—his 'chicken coop.'

The second time was, when he saw two Israelites fighting each other; he tried to mediate and solve their issue. They rejected him and his mediation.

In both cases, Moses had good intentions. However, the posture he was addressing them from was to solve the issue and not to identify with the individuals and why they did what they were doing.

Eventually Moses reached a place in his heart where he identified himself with his brethren and decided to take the right path, as we will read about in the verses below.

Moses responded to both incidents, because when he noticed them, they each triggered something inside him. His destiny or that which he was born to do moved inside him. The same thing that happened to the eagle when it saw another eagle flying, happened to Moses. However, Moses did not have all the pieces together yet.

What Moses went through in his life, is a pattern for each one of us to follow. It was not easy for him. It won't be easy for us. He decided to deny his fake self and take up the 'cross' (suffering and persecution) to fulfill what he was born to do. The verses below, explain everything he went through, in a nutshell:

> By faith Moses, when he became of age (self-awareness), refused to be called the son of Pharaoh's daughter, choosing rather to suffer affliction (identified with others, and picked up his 'cross') with the people of God (self-discovery) than to enjoy the passing pleasures of sin, esteeming the reproach of Christ greater riches than the treasures in Egypt (self-discovery); for he looked to the reward (self-empowerment).
>
> By faith he forsook Egypt, not fearing the wrath of the king; for he endured as seeing Him who is invisible. (self-actualization).
>
> By faith he kept the Passover and the sprinkling of blood, lest he who destroyed the firstborn should touch them.
>
> By faith they passed through the Red Sea as by dry *land, whereas* the Egyptians, attempting to do so, were drowned (self-governance based on the 'God-factor') Hebrews 11:24-29.

I would encourage you to revisit these verses once you finish reading this entire book. Then, try to identify the stage that you are now in, or the stages that you went through in your life in the past. and the ones that you still need to go through:

Chapter 3 | Leaving Your Chicken Coop

_____

_____

_____

Everything Moses needed to fulfill his assignment was already in him. He was not aware of it. Things that happened in the wilderness during that second forty years of his life, made him feel like a loser. He couldn't see anything good in himself anymore. He couldn't believe he could achieve or accomplish anything worthwhile.

Nevertheless the God who deposited the seed of destiny into his spirit, knew all along what was in Moses—he needed another self-discovery. That is what happened at the burning bush experience. Many of us are in that stage in life.

The Seed Analogy

You've tried many things, and nothing worked out the way you thought they would. Now you feel you don't want to try anymore. You accepted where you are now as being 'normal' or your 'fate.'

Notwithstanding, I want to encourage you, by saying, "There is more to life." It doesn't happen by trying harder, but by yielding our *self* to God, and getting rid of the fake self. That yielding is the death process every seed needs to go through if that seed is going to become a tree.

It is our choice, either we can remain as a seed and get eaten up by life, or we can yield and go through the transformation process to become what we were meant to be. Every seed needs to go through this and there is no exception or shortcut.

For a seed to germinate, it needs to be buried in soil, and remain in that state of "rest." It needs to die. However, that death is not the end of it, but only the end of a season and the beginning of a new one. When buried though, the seed is not doing anything, however, there is more change happening inside that seed than ever before.

A seed doesn't become a tree by trying or working harder, the change that takes place first, is inside that seed; and that change requires for that seed to come to a place of complete rest and surrender. This is what each one of us needs to do in order to become what God meant for us. We need to yield to the process.

This is what happened to Moses in the wilderness. It took him forty years to reach that place of rest or to yield. That's when the impossible happened, God showed up. I want to promise you that, when you and I reach that place, He will show up for us. He never fails.

Leaving your 'chicken coop' is to leave your comfort zone, everything that is holding you back and step out into the unknown. Like a seed preparing to germinate, by being buried in the soil. Like that eagle soared up into the air. There is no guarantee. We will need to trust God with the process.

When that eagle left the chicken coop, it was freedom; but it was also scary. It did not know where it was going. The higher it went, the bigger the perspective on life became of what is available and what is possible; which gave that eagle the freedom and the mind-set to choose and do what it was created to do.

This is what needs to happen to each one of us. There is a huge difference in perspective when we look at life from a 'chicken coop,' and looking at it from heaven's perspective.

At some point each one of us will be required to take a leap into the unknown if we are going to fulfill what we were born to do. This is what everyone who ever made a difference on this earth, had to do. We need to fully trust God with our next breath. As long as we try to play it safe and continue to do what we always did, we will continue to have what we always had.

What happens when you read this book is, this book will *read* you. What I mean is, there is a double meaning to everything you are reading here. You will see your whole life as if on a movie screen, you are the lead actor, because this movie is about you. You will be able to identify where you are in life. Your heart and spirit will be bearing witness to what you are reading in these pages. That's how you know this is God-sent.

The Moses Analogy

Before we go into the next step of self-discovery let's look a little deeper to see if there is anything that would hinder us from reaching it.

Moses had two incidents which haunted him for many years. One was the guilt of killing the Egyptian, and the second one was running away from Egypt and the fear of being found out by the Egyptian authorities.

I can imagine Moses living in fear for forty years. This could be one of the reasons when God appeared to him he was not willing to go back to Egypt. He did not want to confront his fear and the fear of death.

What can stop us from experiencing self-awareness and self-discovery

There are two things that can stop us from experiencing self-awareness and self-discovery.

The first is the fear that you are afraid to confront, and the second one is the sin you are hiding from confessing. Neglecting to do this, these two traps will eventually destroy you.

Moses could have been living as a fugitive in the land of Midian, afraid that he would be found out and brought back to Egypt to face justice.

Many live a "fugitive" life emotionally and spiritually. They go to their graves with their fear and sin. They believe nobody will understand, forgive or accept them. The enemy convinced them that they committed some unpardonable sin. They would rather sacrifice their destiny on the altar of self preservation and the fear of rejection.

If your sin or fear involves another person, go to that person privately and talk about it and find closure and peace. Do not make a public spectacle of someone's sin which God already forgave them. Do not bring shame and dishonor to someone's life or family. There is nothing we gain from it. "Do unto others as you would want them to do to you."

This fear and sin become the hooks of Satan that he pulls every time we want to take a step and move forward. The enemy will trigger us into panic mode and then we self-sabotage our seasons and opportunities, and go into hiding again. Decades go by, and life slips away from us.

Rather, let us be honest with ourselves, and then deal with these once and for all; and go on to experience freedom. Do not let it steal another day or season from us.

What is that fear that you have been avoiding to confront? Something about you that you don't want others to know. When and how did it start?

_____

_____

_____

_____

What is the sin, guilt or regret that you are afraid to confess that the enemy is using as a hook to keep you paralyzed ?

_____

_____

_____

Chapter 3 | Leaving Your Chicken Coop

In what areas of your life have you settled for convenience instead of surrendering to your calling?

_____

_____

_____

_____

What would it take for you to fully step away from a life of reaction, performance, or comfort, and walk into your Kingdom assignment with faith?

_____

_____

_____

_____

CHAPTER 4

Self-Discovery

When we decide to become the original, real, or authentic, others with fake selves will feel uncomfortable around us. They will try to lay a guilt-trip on us, saying there is something wrong with us or that we are doing something wrong—just like the flapping of that eagle's wings made other chickens around it uncomfortable.

When you decide to become real and do what God created you to do, it will create some chaos or commotion in the people around you. It could create "Trouble in the Coop." Everyone won't celebrate it. This is normal, so don't lose your peace over it.

They want you to remain where they are. They don't want you to change or cause any disruption to their mundane life in the 'chicken coop.' In fact, the people who were close to you up until that time, may reject and label you. It will bring suffering, and there is no escape from it.

Once we come to the place of self-awareness it makes room for self-discovery. The greatest discovery on earth is self-discovery. Self-awareness has to do with knowing *who we really are,* our *true identity.*

Self-discovery has to do with *why we are here* and *what we possess or carry inside us; and identify the resources and opportunities that are around us.* Until then, we will keep looking elsewhere for the things we need to live, and do what we were created to do.

Once we reach self-discovery, we come to realize that everything we ever needed was right inside us all along. What held us back was the fear and the doubts of our self-generated fake identity.

DNA Example

This is how God starts every life. Every life starts with a seed or a DNA. Our DNA is the best example. Everything we needed to become was coded onto that miniscule DNA that we can't even see with our natural eyes.

It is like a seed. Most of us don't see the tree that is hidden in that seed. We can't see what God coded into our spirit. God doesn't merely see just that seed, but He sees the tree and a forest or an orchard that seed could become. God doesn't focus on our frailties and weaknesses, His focus is on the destiny that He spoke into existence.

Adam and Eve Example

When God created Adam and Eve, the Bible says He blessed them (Genesis 1:28). Adam did not have to do anything to receive that blessing. All he had to "do" was to "be" what God created him to be—His son.

Through that blessing Adam received a deposit inside him—in his spirit, of everything he would ever need. All that Adam needed to do was to discover and manifest what was inside him as life unfolded.

Everything you need right now, is right inside you. But our fake self wants to convince us, saying we don't have what it takes, and it is somewhere else or with someone else. So we spend many years looking

Chapter 4 | Self-Discovery

for this "someone" to come and help us. We keep going around the same mountain, and doing the same old thing. Life gets lost in the process and we forget to actually live.

Religious people tend to say Jesus or God is the answer, but they fail to recognize where Jesus or Christ *is* at the moment. Though He is seated in heaven, He is inside each believer. So the answer to our problems need not come from heaven necessarily, it has to come from discovering Who lives inside us. The solutions to every problem we face are already inside us.

We sing to God and ask Him to pour out His Spirit. He looks at us with pity, and sings a song back at us saying, "*I already poured out My Spirit upon all flesh two thousand years ago. Now wake up to who you truly are and what you have received before it gets too late!*"

Every Sunday morning they wait for Him to show up without realizing He lives inside them 24/7. And the Holy Spirit Who lives inside each believer feels grieved, because they don't recognize Him at all.

Many people wander through life thinking they don't have anything. Or, they complain about the country they were born in, or the financial situation they are in. They think they are poor and label themselves with so many false identities. They were taught that poverty is not having any money. This is not true poverty, that is only one of the results of poverty.

True poverty is life without purpose, a vision, and living in the false identity and fakeness—without the ability to recognize our potential, the resources, and the opportunities that are around us. This is true poverty and the cause of not having any money.

Those thoughts stem from the fake self that was put on to them by their culture, religion, country, or their own experiences. But those things will work as a hindrance only until a person experiences self-discovery. Nothing can stop a person who has experienced self-discovery.

Discovering the King and His kingdom

Self-discovery is about *discovering the King* and *His kingdom* that is inside each one of us. Everything you need to fulfill your assignment is already in your Born Again spirit. Your spirit-man carries the kingdom of heaven, the most powerful and abundant kingdom in the universe.

This kingdom comes with an economy that never crashes; a government that never fails; an education system that empowers and does not enslave; a culture that is made of righteousness, peace and joy; a healthcare system that keeps you healthy all the days of your life; and it comes with everything else you will ever need.

Christ—the Master Key

When you discover the kingdom of heaven you will also discover the keys that unlock or lock everything else. Christ is the Master Key Who unlocks all the treasures of wisdom and knowledge that are out there:

> *In whom are hidden all the treasures* of wisdom and knowledge. (Colossians 2:3)

This is why, when you discover God's kingdom, it changes everything. Your diet will change, your habits and way of thinking and lifestyle will change. Your prayers will change, your dependency on religion, rituals, buildings, and belief systems will change.

We won't need any religions anymore. This is why Jesus told us to "seek first" His kingdom and His righteousness to an audience that was deeply rooted in religion. When we find these, everything we need in life will be added to us. We don't need to go looking for them.

Discovering the God-factor

Nothing can stop an individual who has discovered the kingdom of heaven which is inside them. The potential or the seed they carry, I call discovering the God-factor.

Chapter 4 | Self-Discovery

The greatness you are trying to become and the blessing you are waiting to receive is already inside you in a seed form. This is why you keep envisioning or seeing it with the eyes of your imagination. We call it *a vision* or *a dream*.

The truth about vision or imagination is if something doesn't exist, you can't see it. If you can imagine something, that means it already exists. It might exist in the invisible realm. Everything that pertains to life and creation starts in the invisible realm first.

Adam did not ask God for any blessing. Everything was freely given to him by God. It's the same with each one of us (See Romans 8:32 and 1 Corinthians 2:12). When He blessed him, He deposited in him the seed that contains everything he would ever need. You and I carry the same seed or deposit in our spirit-man.

We are all blessed by God because we are all in Christ, Who is blessed forever and ever. There is no curse, sickness, or poverty in Him.

When we understand this, our prayers will change. We won't be asking God to give us anything, but rather to unlock and discover the mysteries of His kingdom that are within us already.

How is your prayer life now? How much of it is filled with personal needs or wants?

_____

_____

_____

_____

Have you discovered the kingdom that is within you? Explain the experience and what you saw:

_____

Principles of Self Governance

_____

_____

_____

The reason we need to have a self-discovery is in order to discover and identify the following.

Discovering Our Purpose

The Messiah Who came to save us from slavery, told us to seek His kingdom and His righteousness first. Why did He say this? Why did He not say, get a good education, build some good habits, try to become a leader, find a government job, reach your higher self or consciousness, or chase money or success first?

Our existence on earth has to do with His kingdom. We are here because of His kingdom. This is why He told us *what* He said. When we find His kingdom, we will meet the King, and we will discover our true identity and the purpose of our life. Life will make sense for the first time. Fulfillment will come. You will finally feel in your spirit that you are *home*.

We need to discover our purpose. Purpose is the reason for our existence. Why are we here?

Most people go through life without ever discovering their big *why*? They were caught up in the survival mode of life. They don't know how to get out of it.

There are so many benefits of discovering our purpose. Below are some of these:

Do you know why God created human beings and put them on the earth?

CHAPTER 4 | SELF-DISCOVERY

_____
_____
_____
_____

Personalize this, and write down your purpose statement:

_____
_____
_____
_____

God honors purpose

God is the Creator of everything and He created everything for a reason and purpose. When He creates something, He defines its purpose right there and then.

So, when that creation steps into fulfilling its purpose, it draws God's attention.

Have you ever wondered why God is not moved by all the needs in the world? Why doesn't God answer the cry of everyone who suffers? Why doesn't He feed everyone who lives in hunger?

People misunderstand and blame God. God cares about all of His creation. But when something is not doing what it was created to do, by remaining in the place He put them, He is not responsible to take care of them. He is Just in all His ways.

The reason why so many are suffering and living in hunger and pain is because they do not know their purpose. The moment someone discovers their purpose, life takes a new course altogether.

Every other creation fulfills their purpose on its own, except for human beings. God created us with the ability to choose. This is a blessing, but could be a curse at the same time. *We* have a role to play in fulfilling our purpose. It's not simply an automatic thing at all.

Purpose attracts favor

When you step into fulfilling your purpose, it attracts favor from both God and people. Have you ever wondered why good things happen to certain people?

They may not look 'holy' based on our religious standards. It is because of *where they are* in life and *what they are doing*. Nothing happens by chance. There is a law of *cause and effect* and *sowing and reaping* established by God that works for all.

Purpose gives fulfillment

Only when we fulfill what we are born to do, does this bring real fulfillment. Many people with great riches and privilege, still feel empty and miserable. They have no reason to live. Money won't bring fulfillment. Many think otherwise. They think money or not having money is their number one problem. That is a lie.

When you are doing what you were born to do, regardless of the amount of money you have, it will still give you fulfillment.

Purpose brings focus and clarity

Many are not effective and productive because they are trying to do too many things. They are always busy. Twenty years pass by, and they haven't accomplished anything meaningful yet.

Noise and distractions are an enemy of focus and productivity. When you understand your purpose, distraction disappears; you become laser-focused, and clarity comes.

Purpose provides protection

The safest place for a fish is water. The safest place for a plant is to be planted in the soil. Everything God created belongs in a specific place. God created human beings to live in His kingdom.

The best way to stay safe is to do what God created us to do, by remaining in the place He put us.

Purpose brings joy

Because people are not happy with what they are doing or dissatisfied with their work, they go someplace else to have some fun or joy, and waste their money.

There is nothing more fulfilling than doing what you were created or born to do. There is an unspeakable joy that comes when you are fulfilling your purpose. Your joy will not be based on anything material or on the circumstances around you. Joy will spring up from within.

There is not enough room in this book to write about all there is when it comes to purpose. We have an excellent resource—one of our best-selling books—called *Discovering Purpose, Calling and Gifts*. **This book dives deeper into the subject and lays out the Biblical foundations and the framework for fulfilling our calling. To order a copy:**

Are you ready to unlock the secret to your true purpose and experience a transformational journey?

Discovering Purpose, Calling and Gifts

by **ABRAHAM JOHN**

Why will this book change your life?

- You will discover your **true identity** in God and the gifts He has given you.
- You will follow **practical, biblical steps** to activate your purpose and calling.
- You will understand **worship** as a life dedicated to honoring God.
- You will be **empowered** to break through limitations and exercise your **spiritual authority**.
- You will renew your understanding of **biblical truths** to transform your faith and your daily life.

ORDER NOW
www.Treeof-life.com

Our Potential

The next thing to discover is our potential. Everyone has potential. What is potential? Potential is the inherent capacity, ability, or energy that is contained in a person to learn or to do a specific task. In its simplest form, potential is unused energy.

The reason people make excuses about their present condition is because they don't realize their potential, opportunities, and resources that are available to them. They don't want to do anything different. They don't want to put in the effort or make a demand on their potential.

Kingdom Principle

Potential is a kingdom principle. God will not create anything without potential and purpose. Anyone who is poor on the earth today is because they don't understand the principle of potential.

We need to use this potential to develop a skill, specialized knowledge, a business, to raise crops, or anything that is useful.

What are the inherent abilities or gifts the Creator gave you at birth?

_____
_____
_____
_____

What are you doing with them?

_____
_____
_____

Gifts and Skills

We need to identify our natural and spiritual gifts. In God's kingdom, spiritual and natural gifts are equally important. It's like a train, which needs two tracks; and birds, which need two wings to fly; so we need both hands to function properly.

Without our natural gifts, we will not make a lasting impact in society and our nation.

A person who is an expert in a natural gift will at some point need the help of a person who is an expert in spiritual gifts or knows how the spirit world operates in order to navigate his life or business. A person who is an expert in a spiritual gift will need the help of people with natural gifts to conduct his life or ministry.

We are natural and spirit beings, living in both realms simultaneously. We are sent to manifest what is in the spirit (heaven) in the natural world—the earth. This is why God gave us a body and spiritual and natural gifts.

Spiritual gifts are there in order to make what is in the spirit a reality in the natural world, whereas the natural gifts are there to align the natural. also help us to solve problems in both worlds.

God gave us our natural gifts at birth, or a desire or passion to develop certain skills. We need to start using and mastering these as early as possible. Parents play an important role in this.

The pattern every generation must follow

This is what we see in David's life. He had a natural gift or passion for music. He mastered that gift early enough; and by the time he was a teenager, that gift opened the door to the next season in his life for him to reach the palace. This is a pattern every generation must follow.

That was only the beginning. He did not build a life, identity, or career solely based on that gift. A gift or skill is a key that unlocks the door to new seasons in our lives.

The reason why many remain poor is because they have not mastered or developed any skills or gifts. They simply remained "good or nice people," but did not focus on becoming "valuable or effective."

What are the gifts, skills, and passions you have?

_____

_____

_____

What are you doing with these, and how are you maximizing them?

_____

_____

_____

What were your interests or passions while growing up?

_____

_____

_____

Which subject or skill were you naturally inclined to?

_____
_____
_____

What did you do with those desires, passions, and opportunities?

_____
_____
_____

Opportunities

There are opportunities everywhere. However, these don't wait for anyone. We need to recognize and seize the opportunities which come our way. God is faithful in this regard. He is not partial to anyone.

The moment we are ready, opportunities will show up. Like they say, when the student is ready, the teacher shows up.

There are different kinds of opportunities. Some of these will be to learn new things. We need to maximize these as much as we can.

When I was a teenager, I used to see ads in newspapers about learning foreign languages. My heart said, you need to learn these languages. But I did not put in enough effort at that time to learn them. I regretted it later. My excuse was I did not have any money. But I knew if I really wanted to do it, I could have come up with something. Where there is a will, there is a way.

More than thirty years have gone by. As I am writing this book, I am in Chile, a Spanish-speaking country in South America. Spanish was one of those languages that I wanted to learn when I was a teenager. While that did not stop me from coming here, it could have helped me communicate better with the people here.

What opportunities are available to you right now? Assess and identify these, and make a plan to maximize them.

The reason many say they don't know what to do with their lives is because they haven't maximized the opportunities they should have in the previous season of their lives. They did not know they were supposed to do this. They were told that going to school and getting an education is the solution.

What are the opportunities that are around you at the moment that you can maximize?

_____

_____

_____

_____

Kingdom Strategy

Imagine that you were entrusted with an important task but you didn't have the tools or forget the tools. Feeling lost or frustrated wouldn't solve the problem. You need to have the right tools in order to be able to complete the task.

One of the most important kingdom strategies is to be at the right place, at the right time, doing the right thing with the right people. But if we don't have the right tools, we will miss out on everything.

Principles of Self Governance

Gifts and skills are tools which accomplish the task, and the keys which open the doors for us.

If we don't identify and master these early enough, life will simply pass us by.

Our *Gifts and Skills Workshop Manual* is designed to help an individual identify and master the spiritual and natural gifts God gave us.

Relationships

Though God is Sovereign and can do anything He wants to, He chooses to use His children to accomplish His purpose on the earth. The majority of the time He works through people. When God wants to bless you or wants to take you to a new level in any area of your life, usually He sends a person into your life.

Relationships are important in God's kingdom because everything flows through them. Unfortunately the enemy also works through people. Very seldom Satan appears to anyone with a spear in his hands and horns on his head. He is a spirit-being and he also needs physical bodies to operate through on the earth.

We need to recognize the relationships which God sends into our lives. They carry the solutions or the keys you need for this season in your life and to prepare you for the next season. If we neglect to honor and appreciate the people whom God sends, then we may miss out on the blessing they were sent to bring.

Write down all the key relationships that you have right now:

_____

_____

_____

_____

List the toxic and draining relationships which you need to let go of as you are entering into the new season:

_____

_____

_____

Resources we already have

We need to recognize the resources that are available around us. Most are stuck on what they don't have, and so, fail to recognize what they do have. One of the kingdom keys is whatever we need to start what God created us to do, we already have. The Bible says God has given us everything we need for life and godliness (See 2 Peter 1:3).

It could at least be the potential God deposited in us, however, we are not using it to develop any skills or knowledge, but are stuck in a poverty mind-set. Rather, we spend our lifetime making excuses.

Identify and write down the resources that are available to you

_____

_____

_____

_____

Problems

We need to identify the problems that are around us. Opportunities come to us disguised as problems. We are alive and breathing because we carry the solutions to someone's problem or a problem that exists in our society, the earth or the world.

First, we need to solve our own personal problems, spiritual and emotional challenges, and setbacks; until we reach the place where we have a positive outlook on life.

Then, we identify the immediate problems we have around us.

Joseph's example

Joseph was in the prison when he noticed two of his inmates having a bad day. He noticed they looked worried. He asked them what's going on, and they shared their problems. Both had dreams but couldn't understand the interpretation of them.

For Joseph to ask about their well-being, he had to be self-aware first. That prison cell or what others labeled him did not define who he was, his identity, or his future. His identity was based on his true self that God created.

He had already dealt with the rejection and the injustice his brothers and his boss inflicted on him. He did not have a negative attitude nor harbored any bitterness toward them. He was ready to identify with the people and their problems that were in his immediate surroundings, and he was equipped to solve these. This is one of the qualities of a person who has reached self-awareness.

He had the gift that solved their problems. He was rewarded for it later. This is the purpose of gifts and skills. To solve others' problems and to open doors for us so that we can step into the next season of our lives.

When you master a gift or a skill, people will come looking for your service. Your gift or skill is a solution to the problem someone else has. They need what you have to solve their problem.

When you solve their problem they will pay you for your service. The more intense or acute someone's problem is, the greater your reward will be. This is the key to unlocking your provision in God's kingdom.

What are the problems that you can identify in your immediate circle?

_____

_____

Principles of Self Governance

_____

_____

How many of those problems can you solve?

_____

_____

_____

_____

If you cannot solve these, write down why:

_____

_____

_____

_____

What can you do to empower yourself to solve these?

_____

_____

_____

_____

Discover your Niche

Your niche is what makes you unique. This is *how* you are going to solve others' problems. It's the combination of your specific gift, skill, knowledge, and the experience you gained.

Don't waste your experiences and the wisdom you gained from life. Other people need what you have obtained because that is your specialty.

You're one of a kind and created to be an original. It takes courage and determination to live an authentic self.

What makes you unique?

_____

_____

_____

_____

Discover your Audience or Market

Don't live to make everyone happy. If you do, you will end up being a loser. One of the reasons Moses went through all that he went through was to discover who he was supposed to reach or his audience.

Each one of us was created to solve certain problems for a specific group of people. Nobody is a savior of the whole world. There is only one Savior of the world, and that is Jesus Christ.

Moses was supposed to be the deliverer of his people from slavery in Egypt. He was not the deliverer of the whole world.

The Message

The sooner you find the audience you reach and the message, the better life will be. But before you can find your audience and the market, you need to know your message.

Your message is what you are going to tell your audience, what you are offering them. Your message is your life's mission that you are sent to accomplish.

Principles of Self Governance

Moses' message was freedom from slavery. To take the people of God to a land that flows with milk and honey. His message to Pharaoh was to let God's people go. We can see how many times that phrase or mission was repeated in the book of Exodus.

It took me forty years to receive and understand the message I am supposed to share with my audience. Until then, I was preaching what others were preaching.

Don't try to figure out your message. It will come to you at the right time. If you do not have your message yet, you are in preparation to receive one. Your life needs to reflect the message you are sent to deliver. You become the message.

What is the message you are called to deliver to your audience?

_____

_____

_____

_____

Do you know your audience? If so, *who* and *where* are they?

_____

_____

_____

To Know more about our purpose, calling and gifts please read the *Discovering Purpose, Calling and Gifts* **book. To order a copy visit www.TheKingdomNetwork.org**

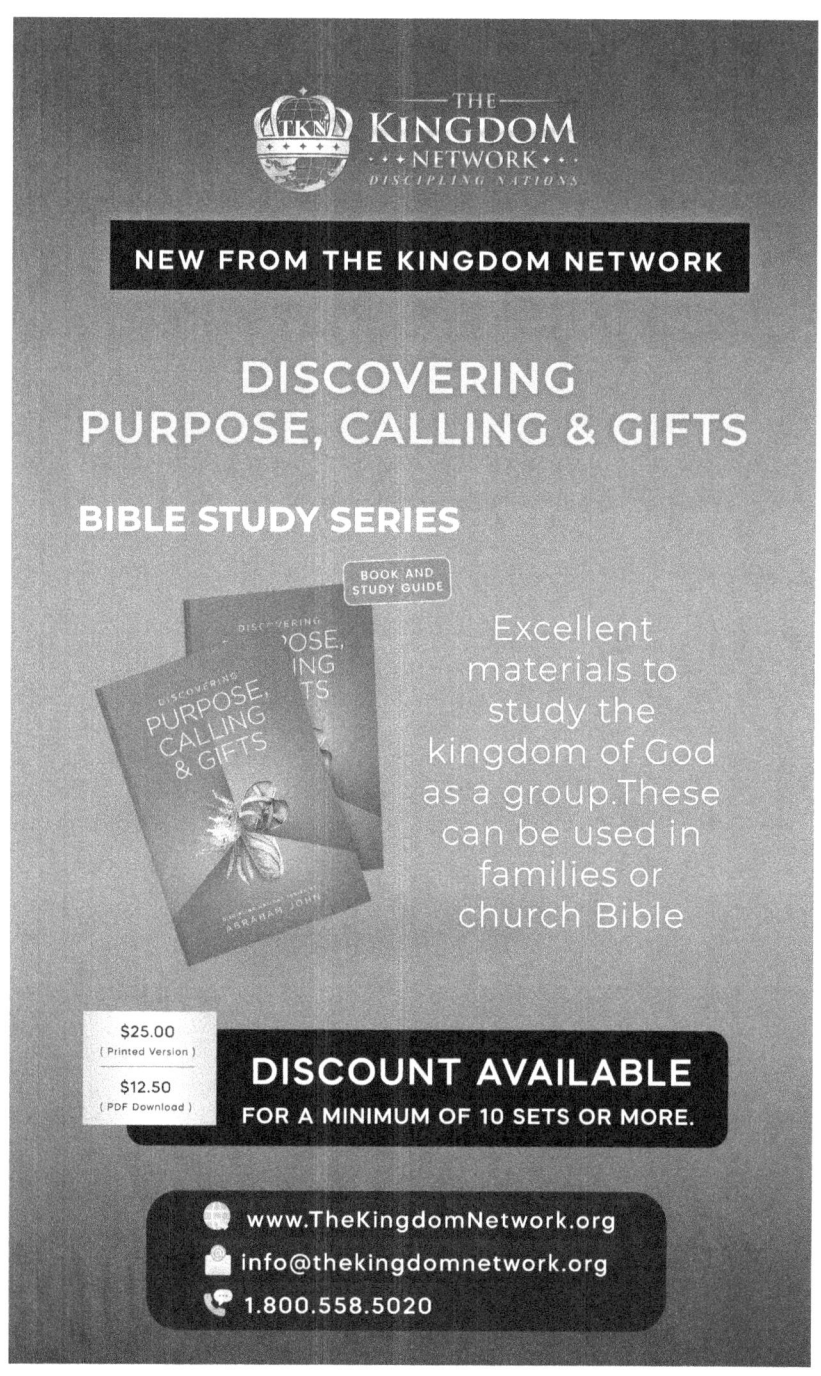

Reflection and Action

What recurring dreams, visions, or inner longings have you dismissed as unrealistic, but now realize may be pointing to your God-given potential?

_____

_____

_____

Are you waiting for something external to change before you act, or are you ready to recognize what God has already deposited within you?

_____

_____

_____

What signs have you seen that God may already be awakening the "seed" inside you?

_____

_____

_____

Are you waiting for everything to be perfect, or are you willing to begin now, with what you already have, and let God multiply it?

_____

_____

CHAPTER 4 | SELF-DISCOVERY

Have you recognized any repeating cycles in your life where you've had opportunities but didn't act? What can you learn from those patterns?

How are your daily choices (work, time, conversations) aligning—or not aligning—with your purpose and identity in the Kingdom?

Do you feel genuine joy in your current work, ministry, or season—or are you merely getting through your days?

Principles of Self Governance

Despite what you have or don't have materially, do you feel fulfilled in your spirit? If not, what may be missing?

_____
_____
_____
_____

In what areas of your life do you feel restless or unfulfilled? Could this be a sign that you are not yet walking in your purpose?

_____
_____
_____
_____

CHAPTER 5

Self-Empowerment

> "Empowerment is not bestowed; it is cultivated through deliberate effort and resilience. By empowering ourselves, we become lighthouses, beacons of hope and inspiration for others. These lighthouses serve as guiding lights, illuminating the path for those who seek to break free from their own limitations."
> – Joseph Keel

Once self-discovery is achieved, the next step is self-empowerment. This stage involves taking control of one's life, making conscious decisions, and embracing responsibility for one's actions.

The statement above reveals everything I would like to say about self-empowerment. When a person takes responsibility for their own life, for what they know or don't know and where their life is at currently, instead of blaming anything or anyone, self-empowerment initiates.

Your external life is only a reflection of your inner-self. The world out there is a reflection of the collective inner-beings of eight billion people. Our inner-self was formed by our belief systems—called *core belief systems*. Those core beliefs were formed in our childhood years.

Everything that happened in our childhood years has impacted our lives. These formed the core belief system about *who we are* and *how we face life* when we become adults. We are not consciously aware of many of the things that happened to us. They are buried deep in our subconscious and unconscious selves.

We were told that our problems were caused by external factors or circumstances or people that bother us. That is not totally true, those circumstances and people only trigger and bring to the surface what lies deep inside us.

The only way to change our outside life is to change our inner being first. This means, changing our core belief system on which our life was built upon. When we do this, we will come to a place of peace with ourselves and God.

Many people are waiting and looking for someone else to come and fix their problems for them. What they don't realize is, that person is not going to show up. They need to take responsibility for what is happening inside them, and find the solution.

The reason we blame our parents, the devil, or anything else is because of what happened to us; and we feel helpless to change things. What we are really struggling with, is we are not able to recognize the root issue. The root issue lies within ourselves, our core beliefs that were formed by what we went through. Blaming the devil or anyone else is only an escape mechanism we developed to feel some kind of control or power over current circumstances.

Before anything can change externally, what needs to change first is our core belief systems. The change needs to begin inside us. This is the main reason why Jesus told us to repent.

Chapter 5 | Self-Empowerment

If there is any *fruit* that is appearing in our life that we are not happy with, know that the problem lies at the *root*, which is hidden. There is no point in beating the branches or the leaves, we need to find the root issue. In order to find the root issue, it will require some serious digging.

Poverty, insecurity, anger, failures, addiction, rejection, fear, over- or underweight, laziness, racism, immorality, corruption, are all fruits. The roots may go back to something that happened or something someone said in our childhood years. Or because we did not receive the love, acceptance and appreciation from our parents, and that little boy or girl is still looking for it from our parents.

The process we all need to go through

Every one of us needs to go through a certain amount of inner-healing and rewiring of our core belief system. No matter which country or religion you were born in, we need to go through this process until our whole being comes into alignment with God and His kingdom. Jesus did not say only a certain people need to repent, but everyone. The moment we are willing to admit this, self-empowerment begins.

Many people live as victims of their circumstances or of where they were born. Others blame what happened to them after they were born. Some others feel stuck with what others did to them.

These are all painful as they can be, but should not serve as a final verdict of our destiny. We should not let these circumstances be the captain of our destiny and the judge over our lives. We were created to overcome those challenges and move into the stage of self-empowerment.

To reach a place of self-empowerment, we need to take responsibility for where we are in life. Once we arrive at self-awareness, we need to accept responsibility for the fake and false self that we were living with and operating from.

Even though it wasn't all our fault for what happened when we were children, once we became self-aware, we need to take responsibility for allowing those things to determine the quality of our lives as long as we did; and are now willing to address or change them, no matter the cost or the pain.

Moses had to make a choice to continue to live in Egypt or leave. Though he felt like he was running away, defeated, or for his life; in the spirit it was a different story. God saw it as an act of faith, as we saw in the verse above. It was the self-empowerment season for Moses.

One thing about self-empowerment is we don't always add new things or skills. Sometimes it is more about unlearning what we learned in the past season or getting rid of the mind-sets and patterns that are holding us back, than learning new things. It's emptying ourselves, rather than filling. We all need to go through this process.

What are the mind-sets and paradigms that you need to get rid of?

_____

_____

_____

_____

What are the new mind-sets and paradigms which you need to develop that will fit the new version of you?

_____

_____

_____

_____

Chapter 5 | Self-Empowerment

Have you accepted responsibility for where you are in life currently?_____

What are the things you were blaming for the state of your life?

_____

_____

_____

_____

When we follow and trust God, even the mistakes we make turn out to be for our benefit. For Moses, killing the Egyptian was a mistake, but God used this to turn around the course of his life.

When you look back at your life, those circumstances and incidents which you thought were the most painful, or the most unfortunate— would be the ones that created the most change or impact in your life.

You will see the benefit these brought to your life. This is part of self-empowerment. If you don't look at it this way, you will remain a victim of your circumstances and what happened to you.

Once we empty ourselves, God will begin to fill us with His wisdom and grace. When we are weak, He will show Himself strong. Moses had to go through this process of emptying.

Self-empowerment means to bring our spirit, soul, and body into full alignment with God and His kingdom. Whatever is not part of His kingdom needs to go *bye-bye*. Then, we learn how His kingdom operates, and apply it in our lives.

Taking responsibility

Below are some of the areas we need to take responsibility for in order to ensure our self-empowerment.

Empowering our body

Human beings are the only creatures which come empty-handed and empty-headed (knowledge) into this world, and leave empty. What I mean is, whatever we know now was taught to us by someone else. Whatever we have now was either given to us or we earned these.

We did not bring anything into this world. We did not come into this world knowing what to eat and how to eat and how to live. If we leave a baby alone for a few days, that baby won't survive on its own.

Our bodies were made for movement. If we don't move our bodies enough, they will start to malfunction. The health of our bodies determines how long we are going to effectively live on the earth. It is important to build both healthy eating habits and an exercise program that fits us.

You need to take responsibility for the health and well-being of your body. Our body is the temple of God on the earth. If we destroy the temple of God, He will destroy us.

Action plan

Do you have healthy eating habits? If not, what needs to change?

_____

_____

_____

Do you exercise on a regular basis? If not, why?

_____

_____

Chapter 5 | Self-Empowerment

Empowering our Soul or Mind

Emotional and mental health is important. We are as productive as our minds. Our mind or brain doesn't understand the past or future. It always functions in the present. We were created to live in the *now* and in the divine flow of love and creativity. Whatever information we put into our mind, it believes is truth, and creates our reality accordingly.

When we live in the past or in the future that is not here yet, our mind doesn't know how to handle this. So, we feel regret or anxiety or fear. We can only maximize the present moment.

What we allow into our mind and thoughts

It is important what we allow into our minds and thoughts. We need to be in charge of our thoughts instead of letting our thoughts take control of our lives. We shouldn't be slaves to our thoughts and emotions, instead we need to be in charge of them. This is very important to understand and practice.

When a person takes responsibility for what's happening in their mind and can control their thoughts and imaginations, they have arrived at a level of maturity where they are ready for *self-governance*.

Our mind contains immeasurable amounts of potential and possibilities. There is not a single human being who lived on the face of the earth who maximized their mind and its full potential. Our brain is still the fastest information processor that exists.

God wants us to be productive in our minds. Some people's minds are clogged just like a pipe or a hose that is clogged. It doesn't produce or come up with anything good. Our mind is like a bird that is shut up inside a cage. The lid needs to come off.

My declaration

I remove the lid off your brain and the limit of your mind. Lay your hands on your head and command it to function as it is supposed to function. Command it to be productive and come up with new ideas, creativity, direction, and solutions.

Read books that empower your mind and those which give you the right kind of knowledge which is key to you fulfilling your destiny. Don't waste your life reading fiction and fables. It may entertain your brain, but doesn't empower you.

How is your thought life? Are you in charge of your thoughts or a victim of them?

_____

_____

_____

_____

How much time do you spend reading in order to learn on a daily basis?

_____

_____

_____

_____

Write down some action plans to train your mind to think what you want it to think _____

_____

_____

Chapter 5 | Self-Empowerment

Empowering our Spirit

We are a spirit-being sent to earth to accomplish an assignment for God's kingdom. Our spirit contains the DNA of God and the DNA of our assignment. It needs to be educated on who we are and regarding our assignment.

Our spirit knows the purpose and our specific assignment. We need to decode what's in our spirit and download it into our mind. This happens through our relationship with God. The more we get to know God and walk with Him, the more we become aware of our spirit, become stronger, and mature.

What do you do to train and empower your spirit on a daily basis?

_____

_____

_____

_____

Financial Empowerment

Most people believe not having enough money is their problem; but they don't understand how money works. In religion we were taught that when someone gives us some money, it is called a blessing or a miracle. That is not how the kingdom economy works.

In the kingdom, we are recompensed for the value we add to people's lives or for the problem we solve. People pay us based on the value we bring or add to their lives. This means, the more valuable we become by becoming specialized in at least one gift, skill, or knowledge, people will pay or reward us accordingly.

Instead of looking for money or waiting for it to show up; spend time making yourself valuable, and money will find you. The more valuable we become the more we will get paid. Now the question is, how do we add value or become valuable? That's what I'll explain in the next point.

God is faithful to give us seeds, it is our responsibility to sow, cultivate, and grow those seeds. He will not do that for us.

What is the gift, skill, or knowledge that you are specialized in?

_____

_____

_____

_____

Do you have a budget or a financial plan? If not, why?

_____

_____

_____

_____

Gifts and Skills Empowerment

We become valuable by mastering gifts, skills, and specialized knowledge. We need to master something or anything. Most people remain a jack of many trades but master nothing. If you watch them they never get ahead financially either.

However, if you look at someone who is prosperous financially, you will also notice they have some special skills, gifts, or knowledge that others don't have. They took the time to master those gifts, skills, or knowledge.

Chapter 5 | Self-Empowerment

Where did they find that gift, skill, or knowledge? They discovered it inside them, took responsibility for their self-empowerment, and invested time and effort in mastering it. It was just a matter of time and they started to prosper; while others remain in the same place, talking or wishing things would change for them.

We need to take personal responsibility for our empowerment. We shouldn't wait for someone else to do it for us. On reaching the age of accountability, it is the responsibility of each individual to decide and come up with a plan for their personal empowerment or development.

What are you specialized in?

_____

_____

_____

_____

What are you doing currently to become more valuable?

_____

_____

_____

_____

The Purposes and Roles of Spiritual and Natural Gifts

God puts desires and passions in our hearts. He brings opportunities in front of us. But He will not make the decisions for us. This is key in developing skills. You focus and do something about that desire, or dream, or passion until that season is over.

From the time a child is born, that child will begin to show interest in certain things or demonstrate certain skills. Those are clues to the wiring or gifting God has programmed into their DNA. Some will have passion to do certain things or to learn something specific. Those are signs or clues of which direction that child should focus and get trained in.

To open doors for us

Gifts and skills are keys that open doors and create opportunities for us. You need to become confident in your gifts and skills. This comes through practicing.

Many people receive prophetic words and then they wait for twenty or thirty years, and nothing happens. Prophetic words are opportunities to partner with God in unlocking prophetic destiny in our lives.

The reason many people haven't seen the fulfilment of the prophetic words they received is because they have not done their homework. They have not mastered what they need to master in order to unlock that destiny. God is waiting for them. They think they are waiting on God.

Every season may require developing new skills or gifts. Gifts and skills are keys that open different doors and seasons in the spiritual and in the natural realms.

To unlock new seasons of our lives

Life happens in seasons. We won't be or shouldn't be doing the same thing all our lives. Even natural life unfolds in seasons. That is why we have childhood, teenage years, and adult life.

Keep in mind, those gifts and skills we develop during our childhood years will be the keys that God will use to unlock the next seasons in our lives. If we do not develop them, then God cannot open those doors for us, because we are not prepared.

Chapter 5 | Self-Empowerment

Thus people miss out the seasons and promotions in their life. Then they wonder why nothing is happening in their life, and why God is not opening any doors for them. It's not God's fault that nothing is happening, because they did not maximize the previous season and the opportunities they had.

We have a role to play and in partnering with God for fulfilling our prophetic destiny. This is what we see in the Bible. We need to know which gift and skill we need to master now for God to open up the next season of our lives. The same pattern follows in every new season. We need to keep moving with God.

We need to discern and know when the time and season is changing. Many people feel frustrated where they are now, because they overstayed their past season. They are frustrated because they have not developed their new gift or skill yet. God is waiting for them.

David might have used his gift in music until his dying day. But that was not the gift that brought provision to his life when he was in his fifties. He needed a whole different set of skills and gifts to prosper as a king and to govern his people and nation.

To solve problems and to bring us before the right and great people

Successful people are attracted to people who can solve problems for them. Successful people have complex problems. They are always trying to make their life simpler and more productive.

Once you master gifts and skills, problems will show up in front of you. These are opportunities for you to step into and address those accordingly.

To unlock kingdom resources and provision for us

When you solve problems you will be rewarded. That's how your provision will come to you.

To manifest God's kingdom and greatness to people around us and nations

Whatever we do, we need to do for the glory of God. When we do something extraordinary to the people around us and nations, make sure we give Him all the glory and praise. God is very particular about this.

To demonstrate God's glory and goodness to others

God is a good God. How do we or people experience His goodness? It is when His children demonstrate His goodness and grace to others who are in need of it.

To bring souls into God's kingdom

When we are walking in our purpose and calling, others will be attracted to us. They want to be part of something bigger than themselves. They will want to know the God we serve.

Important to know

Don't try to build your whole life based on a gift that was only meant to open a new season in your life.

In the life of David we see that God used his gift for music and his skill of shooting a stone with a sling, which caused all of the above-mentioned blessings to manifest in his life. When he stepped out to use his gifts and skill, these opened new doors for him to step into his new season and destiny.

He solved the problem, by killing the giant; while his gift in music soothed the demonic oppression of king Saul. Each unlocked a new season of his life, as he went from being a shepherd to serving the king in the palace; which unlocked kingdom provision and resources for him. He married the king's daughter and became part of the royal family; which

Chapter 5 | Self-Empowerment

created thousands of followers who sang his and God's praises. This is the power and purpose of natural and spiritual gifts.

We see the same things happening in Joseph's life. In his case God used the spiritual gift to unlock all the above-mentioned blessings upon his life. However, once he reached the palace, he shifted toward using his natural gifts of administration and governing to launch the largest farming and construction projects (building store houses and distribution centers all across Egypt) in the history of the nation.

In the case of Esther, it was her authentic feminine nature and qualities of a virtuous woman that attracted the king. He married her, and she became his queen. There would have been many other women more physically attractive and glamorous than Esther who came to the royal interviews for a new queen.

Whatever season you are in now, assess and find out what you need to learn and master now in order to prepare for the next season. What are the opportunities that are available to you now?

Don't get blinded or distracted by the responsibilities or become comfortable because of job security or distracted by the challenges of the current season. There is a hidden opportunity in every crisis or challenges we face in life.

Some people wait until they are late in life to do what they should have done or learned when they were in their childhood years. Imagine David trying to focus on his music skill when he was thirty? He wouldn't have reached where he was.

There is nothing wrong with learning or developing a skill at any time or age in our lives. Every skill and gift we develop, have their specific role and function, and are connected to specific assignments and seasons of our lives.

Imagine if Joseph tried to build a business or ministry around his dream interpretation gift? Making appointments for Egyptians to come to him every morning to receive interpretation for their dreams. He could have made a living from it, but not necessarily fulfilled his kingdom assignment. Don't short circuit your destiny by getting stuck or settled in one particular season of your life, because a particular gift worked for you in that season and brought provision to you. You need to move on with God and His timing for your life.

In order to establish God's kingdom on earth we need people who are mastered and matured in both spiritual and natural gifts and skills. We need people who are sensitive to God's timing and seasons and are willing to change and learn new things. Otherwise we will be like a bird trying to fly with one wing and won't get anywhere. We will be going around in circles. This is what the church has been doing for the past two thousand years.

How did the saints in the Old Covenant manifest God's kingdom and will on earth?

It was by using their gifts and skills. First they established a nation. Then implemented each component of a kingdom as God gave them directives through Moses.

Are you willing to invest time and resources in order to master your gift and learn some new skills to advance God's kingdom on earth?

That is what Esther, Daniel and the disciples had to do. God is waiting for us.

Religion told us that we are waiting on God and praying for a move of God or for revival. God is always moving. He never sleeps nor slumbers. When we wake up to the reality of who we are and what we have been given, and use our gifts and skills properly and responsibly, we will see the same result those people saw in Bible times.

Chapter 5 | Self-Empowerment

It takes only some three to five years to develop and master a skill or a gift. Imagine how many years we have already spent in our lives. Compared to that, five years is nothing. It would be the best investment you will make in your life.

What are the things you can do now to go to the next level in your gift or skill?

Of all the workshops we have prepared, my favorite one is *Mastering Gifts and Skills*. Because without these we would not make it in life, no matter how spiritual or pious we may be.

Many people heard the gospel of the kingdom and believed it; but wonder why the provision Jesus promised in Matthew 6:33 is not coming to them.

It is because they are not walking in their calling using their gifts and skills. Hearing and believing is one thing, but *doing* is what matters the most.

We have prepared this Workshop to help you identify your natural and spiritual gifts. Pease see next page for more details.

Relationship Empowerment

Why is the number of failed marriages increasing daily? Because people get married or enter into relationships for the wrong reason and motives.

We should only think about getting married after we've gone through the self-awareness and self-discovery processes mentioned in this book; and then marry a person who fits our vision.

Imagine "two fake selves" getting married and trying to live together while still trying to figure out life. There is nothing "real" in that relationship. Even the fights they have are not real, because they will be fighting about the wrong things; or, merely dealing with the symptoms.

They can't identify the root issue. They fight about how to squeeze the toothpaste and on which side of the bed they should sleep. Life keeps going around in circles and cycles. They get worn out and want a time out. Or one partner will end up leaving or cheating, and the relationship will sadly come to a screeching halt.

Only those two individuals who have gone through the self-awareness and self-discovery processes should think about getting married. Then they should work together on self-actualization; because they will have something real to talk about, and a goal, a vision, values, and principles to live by; and something to look forward to in life.

People need something worthwhile to live for, to fight for, and to achieve in life. They need a reason to wake up in the morning other than the mundane same old things like bills to pay.

Two souls who have gone through the self-awareness and self-discovery processes have something worthwhile to fight for. They are not fighting each other, but they join forces together to fight the forces that are hindering their purpose, mission, and advancement in life.

What happens when two fake selves get married is they will start fighting to change the other person. They will try to mold and conform the other person to their fake self. When in reality they are the one that needs to change.

The reason they are trying to change the other person is that the other person is making their fears and insecurities uncomfortable for them. The only way to keep their fears and insecurities, is to conform the other person to believe and do exactly the way they believe and do.

When was the last time when we were "fully present" for someone without any personal agenda or motive?

Instead of trying to impose on others what we believe, our view of what they should change or do; trying to convince them how smart we are, or pretending we have the answers to their problems; we think all they need to do is just listen to what we say and do what we say. This is not what most people are looking for.

Being Self-aware

When we are self-aware we are not striving to achieve or make something happen anymore. We are fully present for the other person, who is our neighbor or our partner. We will be able to listen not to fix them or change anything but to identify with their pain and situation.

When we are self-aware we will not be treating people as mere commodities, but as fellow citizens and a family member. When we love our neighbor as we love ourselves, that neighbor becomes our family member.

When we are self-aware of who we truly are, we will not be trying to win anyone over, or make people join our cause or church. We will be joining hands and hearts and facing the world and its challenges together.

When we are self-aware we won't have enemies, even if we do temporarily, we will be able to love them. True love wins hearts and changes them.

Chapter 5 | Self-Empowerment

The world is filled with people who are pretending to be someone that they are not. They are trying to be something that they are not supposed to be. They are running from their fears, insecurities, rejection, pride, ego, nationalism, religiosity, etc. They don't want to face reality, and they don't want to face their real selves.

They keep on running until a crisis hits, which is supposed to facilitate self-awareness. If they don't get it the first time, they have to go through it again and again.

What is the status of your current personal relationships?

Do those relationships fit your vision and where you are going in life?

Are those relationships draining you emotionally and financially, toxic, or empowering?

Are you growing together closer, and preparing for the next season of your life? Or, are you growing apart?

Everything fails or succeeds because of relationships. It is important for each person to go through a healing process before they enter into long term relationships, especially marriage.

Many marriages fail because people are not trained or equipped properly. Our *Healing Relationships* Workshop Manual has been prepared to train and give each person the knowledge and skills they need to have a fulfilling relationship. Please see next page for more details.

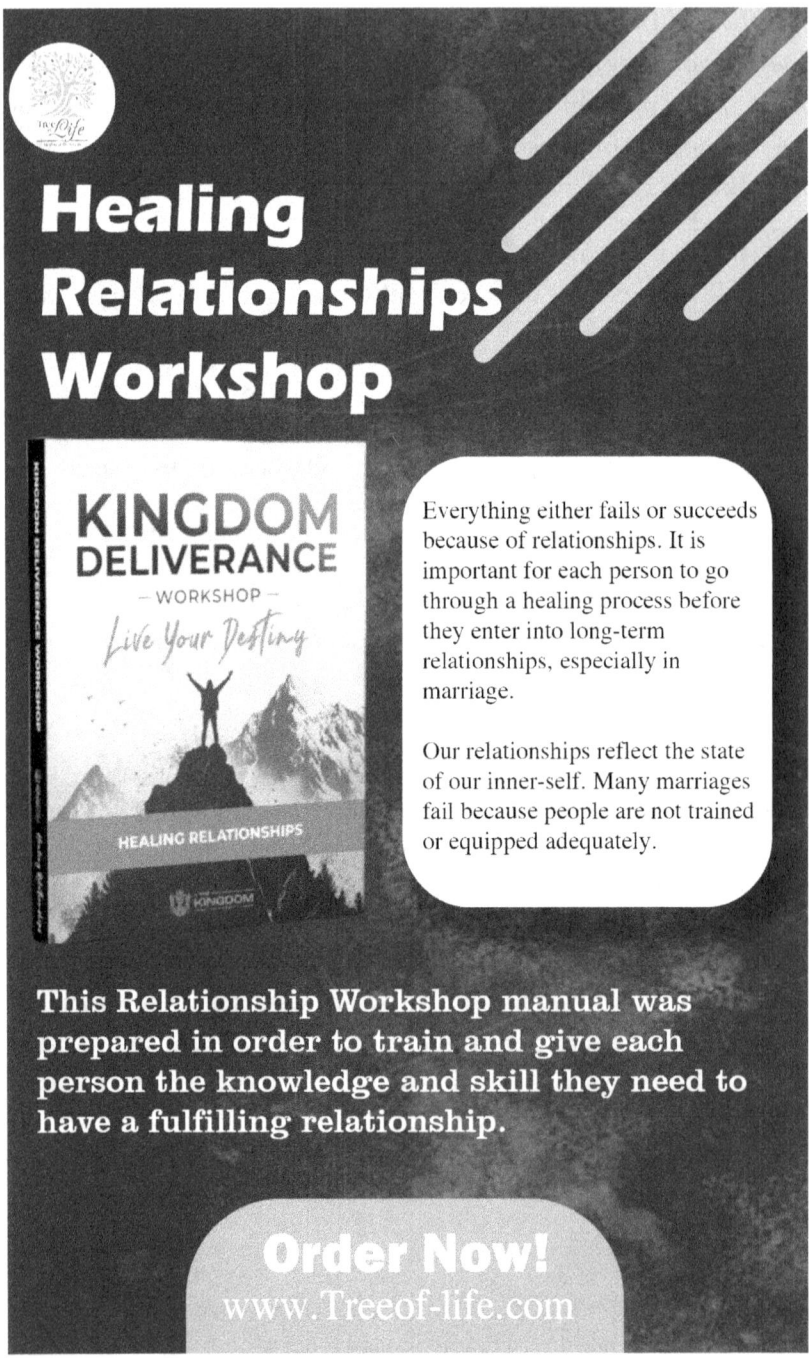

CHAPTER 5 | SELF-EMPOWERMENT

Education Empowerment

We have a world full of "educated" people. But is the world any better and safer now than before?

What we need is a whole new system and curriculum of education in order to train people to reach a place where they govern themselves. The education has to be geared toward taking an individual through the process of self-awareness, which leads to self-discovery, which leads to self-empowerment, which leads to self-actualization, and then self-governance.

Education needs to start by answering the three fundamental questions which every individual needs to find. These are: "Who am I? "Where did I come from?" "Why am I here?" When we are ready to answer those three questions with confidence, that is the day we are ready to live for the first time.

Until that happens everything we receive and call education is geared toward enslaving us to a system. Just because we have a degree from a university doesn't mean we are educated.

We may be qualified to get a job or to offer some service, based on the standard set by the government. However, even those people who have a degree and are doing a job, are asking those same fundamental questions within themselves.

Until each individual reaches the state of self-governance, the education process should continue. They will need to be part of some form of ongoing training in their communities. This must be set in place and is particularly essential in order to reach this form of government that I am writing about in this book.

Education must not be geared toward getting a job in order to make a living, but to produce responsible citizens who have gone through the process mentioned in this book, and are able to govern themselves.

If someone fails or makes a mistake, there should be systems and governance set in place in each community to implement proper discipline, and to take that individual through the training again, until they "get it."

In this way we won't need any prisons or detention centers. There will be people who are trained to deal with such situations and individuals. We need to create and implement systems and processes to help individuals to achieve this goal.

Was the education you received geared toward getting a job, status, title, or personal empowerment to fulfill your destiny?

_____

_____

_____

_____

What can you do to start a self-awareness program for your family or in your community?

_____

_____

_____

_____

Time Empowerment

Whether we live in Africa or America, we all have equal amounts of time in a day. However, we are not all at the same level of productivity, which is based on how effectively we use our time.

Time management is extremely important for self-empowerment. The effective way to manage time is by creating and following a schedule.

Chapter 5 | Self-Empowerment

Again, don't be rigid and uptight; if you do, you will lose the joy of living. Always make room and time to relax and reset. Time was created for us, not the other way around.

In general, there are three groups of people: The first group are those who make things happen, by fulfilling their assignment. The second group are those who talk about what happened. And the third group, are those who wonder what happened.

Do you invest, spend or waste time?

_____

Do you follow a schedule, have a "to do list," or an action plan?

_____

_____

_____

_____

How long have you been living in the current situation wishing something would change?

_____

_____

_____

_____

What action have you taken other than wishing your current situation and reality will change?

_____

_____

Principles of Self Governance

_____

_____

What are the excuses/lies that you keep on telling yourself and others for the reason you can't change or improve?

_____

_____

_____

_____

CHAPTER 6

Self-Actualization

> **Actualization is the realization or the fulfillment of one's talents, potential, and calling. It is the manifestation of our purpose in the real or natural world. Until this happens, our purpose and calling remain only in the idea stage.**

In Biblical terms this is called entering your Promised Land or a place of abundance. However, before we step into actualization, we must make sure we have the following things ready:

Plan

A plan is a simple step by step process of how to achieve your goal or dream. You may not have the whole plan from start to finish, but at least start, having a daily plan; and then build that into a weekly, monthly, and then a five-year plan. If you don't have a plan, know that you are planning to fail.

Preparation

Attach more importance to preparation, rather than to the goal itself. This is where the real growth happens. While preparing we learn new things, build character, values, and consistency.

Principles and Values

We live in a world which is full of corruption, greed, and dishonest people. We need to decide how we are going to navigate through situations—what kind of principles and values we are going to keep and follow.

The core of our life and how we function needs to be rooted in godly principles and values. If we compromise and try to take short cuts, we will short-circuit our destiny.

Partnership

We were not created to live life alone. We cannot achieve what we are called to do alone. We are social beings, and we don't have everything we need in order to fulfill our assignment. The bigger the assignment, the greater the number of people we will need to partner with.

Though we need the help of others to fulfill our calling, we need to be extra careful just who we allow into our personal orbit or the inner circle. Not everyone has the same intentions and good motives as we do. Most people come to us for what they can get out of us. They don't care about our vision or goals. The sooner you detect them, the better you can safeguard the mission.

Patterns

There are patterns to everything in life. A pattern is an example or a system that is common to everyone. There are others who have gone before us from whom we can learn.

Chapter 6 | Self-Actualization

In our journey of fulfilling our assignment we will make plenty of mistakes. It is easier to learn from other's mistakes than from making our own.

Take Action

The final, but the most important step, is to take action. Now that you have a clear understanding of *who* you are and *why* you are here, it's time for action. Until we take action, nothing happens. Many people stay in the talking stage and never move into the action stage. Then they wonder why nothing is happening and why life is not improving for them.

In order to fulfill our assignment, and make any difference on the earth, self-discovery is not enough. Once we discover our purpose, potential, opportunities, resources, and problems; we need to move on into the next step of *actualization*.

Actualization is making our purpose and potential a reality; bringing these from the concept stage, to manifestation; by transitioning them from the invisible realm to the visible realm; from the idea stage, to having a *product* that we can see, touch, and use; which should eventually produce a stream of income for us.

I would say actualization is the most difficult part. This is where most of us make mistakes and determine whether we are going to make it or quit in the middle. Many go up to the level of self-discovery. They have a dream or a vision or a prophecy they have been waiting for to happen. But they don't know what to do to take their dream, vision, or idea from the thought realm to the material realm.

As long as our vision and dream remain in the invisible or thought realm it's not going to benefit anyone or make any difference. Our cemeteries are full of unrealized dreams, ideas, businesses, and inventions. People took them to the grave either because they did not know what to do with them or it was too scary for them. Probably the *chickens* around them talked them out of it.

We can delay God's purposes by not being ready. The Israelites had to spend thirty extra years in Egypt because Moses was not ready. God told them they will be in Egypt for only four hundred years. But later, it stated that they were there for four hundred and thirty years. I believe this is because Moses was not ready to fulfill his assignment.

When we prepare and actualize the vision God has for us, it will transform us from inside out. It clears out all dross and the attitudes which are not aligned with God's kingdom; and that fake self that we all inherited or formed in us while growing up, will fall away.

The Bible calls this fake self an *old* self. This old or fake self needs to die completely. It will not die easily because it's part of our very being and our daily life. Getting rid of it is like dying and coming back to life again as a different person with a new attitude and personality. It is like the process where a caterpillar needs to go through in order to become a butterfly. The sad news is, our old or fake self will not die in one single death, we may have to die a thousand deaths in order to recognize this and surrender it.

Moses had to go through this process. It took him eighty years to complete this process. Categorically forty years. Forty years is the span of a generation. Before he left Egypt he was a prince, who was trained in all the arts and wisdom of Egypt. When he returned to Egypt after forty years he was a mouthpiece for God. What happened in between is the transformation that I am talking about.

The fake self he inherited from Egypt as the prince of Egypt, had to go. To begin with, he was not an Egyptian. A fake identity was imposed on him by Pharaoh's household; which formed a mind-set and taught him all kinds of skills and techniques. He could have been a military general or second-in-command to the Pharaoh. Egypt was his 'chicken coop.' It took him forty years to recognize who he really was.

Moses had to go through every step I am talking about in this book on self-governance.

Chapter 6 | Self-Actualization

First was self-awareness. Imagine the shock he had when he realized for the first time that he was a Hebrew being raised up by Egyptians. The parents who he thought and called were his, were not his real parents.

The food he ate and the clothes he wore did not taste and fit right. The language he spoke and the culture he grew up in felt like a misfit. I can imagine Moses with this unsettling feeling inside him all long, like something is not right somewhere. But he couldn't identify what was wrong. He did not reach that place of self-awareness easily.

What are you doing to manage or soothe this unsettling feeling that you feel inside you? What are you doing to mask your fake self? Sports? Religion? Titles? Addiction? Politics? Chasing success? Money? Nationalism? Or something else?

Moses often noticed his Egyptian mother and others in his immediate circle of relationships whispering to each other. He knew something was off. They knew who he was, but they did not dare to tell him the truth because of the benefits he brought them or the hope they placed on him. They were afraid that if they told him the truth, he might turn against them and stop producing what he was doing, or run away. They had invested a lot in him. So, the benefits were mutual.

Things happened, and life did not go as he thought and planned. Can anyone reading bear witness to this? Did your life go the way you desired and dreamed?

When the time came that Moses had to leave Egypt, it was not easy for him. He had to give up everything he thought was life and real to him. He had to walk away from everyone he thought was his family. The pain was too much to express and the price was too high, but a destiny was at stake.

Either he could keep his fake self, fake family, fake identity, possessions, profession, titles, and privileges; and sacrifice his destiny; or, he could give all that up, and gain something real and eternal of value.

Are you willing to leave your *Egypt*? Your 'chicken coop?' Or, will you find a reason to stay, and waste your destiny? The benefit of giving up the fake self and identities is we receive the real ones. It took Moses forty years to get rid of the fake self. Everything he knew and believed had to go. That is called *repentance*. He had to go back to the beginning.

Repentance

Repentance is unlearning everything we've known until that moment when we start learning the truth about ourselves, God, and everything and everyone around us. The truth we learn and understand and apply, will set us free.

Everything out there is faking it

Every religion, current church system, governments, politics; you name it, everything that is out there, are all fake.

The church I grew up in and was so passionate about for the first thirty five years of my life, I discovered had nothing to do with the New Covenant, Jesus or what He did or what He said. It couldn't even save the people who were following that system. We were all so zealous about it, thinking that was what God wanted from us. Every Sunday we were trying to make God happy. We were preaching a different Jesus and were manifesting a different spirit—*a religious spirit*.

How do we know whether we are playing religion, serving another Jesus, and have received a different gospel and a different spirit?

Through what we do if the kingdom of God is not manifesting on the earth in some way or form; then, whatever we're doing, is based on deception.

If we are not occupying any territory; if the earth is not turning to heaven; if God's will is not being done on earth as it is in heaven, then

Chapter 6 | Self-Actualization

whatever we do, no matter how zealously we do it, like Paul did before his conversion, it's a waste; and it is based on a lie.

The concept of God most people have in their life is based on the religion they were brought up with. God is not religious. He did not create any religion. We were not created for any religion.

We created all the religions; including Christianity, Judaism, Catholicism, and Islam. A person needs religion only until they have a relationship with God, and discover His kingdom and their true identity.

Moses had to reach a place where he only did what God wanted him to do. All his ambitions and aspirations built on his fake self, died. When the time came for him to do what he was born to do, he didn't even want to do it anymore.

He thought he was unprepared or missed it. What he did not realize was, everything he needed to do and what he was born to do, was already inside him.

The older we get, the more we realize that everything we thought we needed emotionally or believed we needed had to come from someone else, was already inside us. Every breakthrough we receive is a deeper journey into ourselves—a deeper journey into the treasures God has deposited in our spirit-man.

Moses did not need what he learned in Egypt. In fact, it was the very thing that stopped and robbed him from doing what he was born to do for decades.

The majority of times, what is stopping you and me, is not the enemy; it is the unbelief and self doubt in what God has already deposited in us. Many people think what Moses learned in Egypt, the military strategies and techniques, all played a role in taking the people of Israel out of Egypt. It was not so.

If you look closely, when God appeared to him at the burning bush, he was at the end of his hope. He did not want to go back to Egypt. In fact, he did not want to do anything great or different other than feeding those sheep. He believed he was not qualified or missed his chance in life.

When he received the call of God, he did not feel, *yes;* or said, I can do this, hey, I am ready and have been waiting for this moment all my life, now I am going to put all the training I received from Egypt to use. That was not his response at all. It was just the opposite.

Even after he brought the people of Israel out of Egypt into the wilderness, he did not go out fighting any battles leading an army. When the people of Israel went to battle, he was at the backside of the desert on a rock fighting a different kind of battle. He was praying or interceding for his people.

We do not see an Egyptian military general in Moses, but *a kingdom general.* A kingdom general is the one who only does what his King commands him or her to do, and how to do it.

The Bible says when the people of Israel came out of Egypt they came out as an army. This army was not an ordinary army. They did not have any sophisticated weapons. They were called an army because of who their captain was.

Their captain was not any human trained in Egypt. The Captain of this army was none other than the Lord God Almighty, the Lord of Hosts is His name. He was fighting the battles for them. In fact, the most mentioned name of God in the Bible next to *Elohim,* is the name *Lord of Hosts* (armies) or *Jehovah Sabaoth.*

The greatest lesson we all can learn

What Moses did not realize was, he had everything he needed to go and deliver the people of Israel from Egypt. He had to unlearn everything

Chapter 6 | Self-Actualization

Egypt taught him, and learn to depend and trust God completely for everything. This is the greatest lesson anyone can learn in this life.

When we complete the process of getting rid of the fake and false self and identities, we learn the art of self-governing. We are ready to be governed by God.

When we arrive there, nothing else matters. Nobody needs to tell us what is wrong and what is right. The God Positioning System (GPS) inside us (our spirit) becomes so attuned to its Creator, we will only do what we sense in our spirit, and what He wants us to do.

We will not be led by our flesh (ambition, jealousy, competition, greed, regrets, and selfishness) anymore. All the problems we have on the earth today are because most people are led by their body and its emotions.

Lying, cheating, murder, theft, immorality, corruption, wars all come from the old or the fake self. These are the work of the flesh. Flesh is the other synonym for the fake or false self or the old self.

The purpose of actualization is to transition an individual from being a consumer to becoming a productive one. The purpose of actualization is to transform that person from their fake self to the real self and to their true identity.

To transition from benefit-seeking citizens, to responsible citizens.

To transition from dependent, into interdependent.

To transition from blaming others, to taking responsibility.

To transition from passing through life, to fulfilling purpose.

To transition from survival mode, to living intentionally.

To transition from building a kingdom of self, to becoming a nation-builder.

To transition from living somewhat, to living intentionally.

Fulfilling a God-given Dream

Many people have a big dream. However, they don't realize what it takes to fulfill it. Having a dream is only the first step. It doesn't guarantee anything. If the dream or the calling is from God, He is more committed to helping us fulfill it than we are. If we don't fulfill a God-given dream, then it is His kingdom that is at a loss.

One of the most important things to keep in mind in order to accomplish what we are called to do, is everything is going to take longer than we thought or planned; and nothing happens in life when we want it to. Many people feel frustrated and give up.

One valuable piece of advice I can give you, is don't give up no matter what happens or how many mistakes you make in the process. Remember, it took Moses eighty years to prepare, and another forty years to do what he was called to accomplish.

One thing about anyone who did anything worthwhile in life, is they made many mistakes or failed multiple times. People who find fault in others or claim they haven't made any mistakes in their lives, are those who never did anything different or significant.

Another important thing to keep in mind is when we think we are ready to do something, that means we are not ready. That may sound odd, but it's a fact. What we feel is only a desire for the flesh, we don't have the capacity nor the maturity to do it. We are ready when the flesh doesn't want to do it anymore.

How many of you wished you had a life coach or a mentor to guide, advise, and lead you in fulfilling what you are called to do?

I understand not everyone can afford a life coach. So, we have prepared a workbook or manual that can help an individual step by step how to

Chapter 6 | Self-Actualization

fulfil their purpose. In order to know more on how to actualize your purpose and potential, please place your order for our *Purpose and Calling* Workshop Manual.

Reflection and Action

What would "starting over" in alignment with God's Kingdom look like for you, and what is keeping you from taking that step?

_____
_____
_____

Have you confused your current life with your real life? What if what you think is life… is actually a counterfeit?

_____
_____
_____

If you continue living as you are now, will you fulfill the purpose for which you were sent to this earth?

_____
_____
_____

What are you afraid of losing that's stopping you from gaining what is real, eternal, and aligned with Heaven?

_____
_____

Chapter 6 | Self-Actualization

If God asked you to do something that went against everything Egypt taught you, would you obey? Or would you hesitate because it feels unfamiliar?

_____

_____

_____

_____

Are you ready to live from the inside out, governed by God's Spirit rather than external systems or expectations?

_____

_____

_____

_____

Do you carry shame or regret from past decisions that still hold you back? What would it look like to surrender these as part of your training ground?

_____

_____

_____

_____

CHAPTER 7

Self-Government

> "The end of law is not to abolish or restrain, but to preserve and enlarge freedom." – John Locke

When a person goes through all the above steps and processes, they will arrive at a place or state in their spirit, soul, and body that was intended by God for them from the beginning.

They will start to live from within, not based on external circumstances or their feelings. They will be so self-disciplined that they will be ready to enter a phase in their lives called *self-governance*.

There could be some exceptions. If you try to control or scrutinize these people, they will feel resentment in their hearts toward whoever is doing it. Because they know the price they paid to reach where they are, and they are not trying to do something evil intentionally. They might make mistakes or things could go wrong by oversight, but they will be willing to admit and correct these quickly.

This is the easiest and most fulfilling stage in life. You will have all the systems and processes put in place, and have enough people and resources available to help and manage what you are doing. People who have reached the place of self-governance, will have a disciplined self.

These souls will:

- **Live from their spirit** – They will be living from their spirit, not from their body. Our spirit came from God. Some people are misguided, and they will go into all kinds of illusions about their spirit. They will try to deny their spirit and call it higher self or higher consciousness.

- **Live in the spirit** – They will be in a constant flow of divine grace, revelation, and inspiration. There won't be any hindrances or blockages. If these come, they will be temporary. They will function as a conduit of God to manifest on the earth what is in heaven.

- **Walk in the spirit** – Spiritual life will not be limited to religious exercise inside any religious buildings on a particular day anymore. They will live and function as a temple of God on the earth 24/7. Awareness of our spirit and spiritual life will be as natural as any other aspects of life. That is called *walking in the spirit*. We will function as an Ambassador of God from heaven to earth.

- **Fruit of the spirit** – When we walk in the spirit, the fruit of the spirit will begin to manifest in and through our lives. What is the fruit of the spirit? ***"But the fruit of the Spirit is love, joy, peace, longsuffering, kindness, goodness, faithfulness, gentleness, self-control. Against such there is no law."***
– Galatians 5:22-23 NKJV

Please pay attention to the last part of the above verse. This entire book is about that single line. Self-control or self-governance is mentioned as part of the fruit of the spirit, against such there is no law. When we live in the spirit, walk in the spirit and demonstrate the fruit of the spirit, we will be self-governed and there is no longer any need for a law or rules or regulations.

Chapter 7 | Self-Government

The last part says *against such there is no law*. In other words, such a person is not governed by any rules and regulations, or by any external forces.

> **"...for where there is no law there is no transgression."**
> Romans 4:15

This means, once we are living in the spirit, by manifesting the fruit of the spirit, we are not governed by any do's and don'ts. Once we are in Christ we are no longer governed by the law of sin and death. We need to be governed by a higher law, which is called *the law of the Spirit of life,* and *the law of love*. These are heavenly or spiritual laws.

> **"...sin is not imputed when there is no law."** Romans 5:13

Those who are living by the law of the Spirit of life are able to govern themselves. When we walk in the spirit demonstrating the fruit of the spirit, we will not do any harm or any evil toward our neighbor. We will not steal, lie, cheat, kill, or envy. Thus, there won't be any crimes, and there won't be any need for prisons.

> *Owe no one anything except to love one another, for he who loves another has fulfilled the law. For the commandments, "You shall not commit adultery," "You shall not murder," "You shall not steal," "You shall not bear false witness," "You shall not covet," and if there is any other commandment, are all summed up in this saying, namely, "You shall love your neighbor as yourself." Love does no harm to a neighbor;* **therefore love is the fulfillment of the law**. – Romans 13:9-10

The law of love is the fulfillment of every commandment, constitution and laws of the earth and the Bible. When a person walks in the spirit, they will walk in love. Love is one of the fruits of the spirit.

Now, the question is, *what is love*? Below is the best definition of love ever written:

Love endures with patience and serenity, love is kind and thoughtful, and is not jealous or envious; love does not brag and is not proud or arrogant. It is not rude; it is not self-seeking, it is not provoked [nor overly sensitive and easily angered]; it does not take into account a wrong endured. It does not rejoice at injustice, but rejoices with the truth [when right and truth prevail]. Love bears all things [regardless of what comes], believes all things [looking for the best in each one], hopes all things [remaining steadfast during difficult times], endures all things [without weakening].

Love never fails [it never fades nor ends]. – 1 Corinthians 13:4-8 AMP

If you want to know what love looks like in person or when it manifests in the natural realm, look at the life of Jesus Christ, what He taught and how He lived. He is the embodiment of love. For God is love.

When a person has an encounter with Jesus or God they need to have an encounter with true love. This does not happen most of the time because of people's religious orientations.

The purpose of salvation is to become one with God again. We were separated by the fall. God reconciled us, things on earth, and the world back to Him through the cross (read Romans 5:10; 2 Corinthians 5:19; Ephesians 1:10; Colossians 1:16, 19-20).

In Christ, once you are saved you become one with God, aligned with heaven and everything He created. Whatever is in heaven can now manifest on the earth through you as a "saved" person. Things on earth will begin to change and transform as you fulfill what you were called to do.

We incorporate the whole creation back to heaven and to Christ, by appropriating what has been made available to us in Christ. This is God's eternal plan and purpose.

Chapter 7 | Self-Government

When a person actualizes his or their purpose and fulfills their God-given assignment (calling), that person reaches a level of maturity in their spirit. They don't need to be told what to do or what not to do anymore. They are governed by their spirit which is connected and is one with God. I call this *self-governance*.

They don't become perfect, but instead mature enough to keep and correct themselves, and accept responsibility for their wrongs, and make corrections when they make a mistake. These are responsible citizens, and they are an asset to any country or community. They need to be treated with respect.

They don't need to be scrutinized, what they need is an accountability and an auditing system. They need to be released, and systems of governance need to be put in place for them to manifest their limitless potential.

We need to establish governing bodies and accountability partners in every community made of elders and people that are matured and responsible. We need governors, courts, judges, etc.

Have you noticed the area or community where the rich people live? The surroundings are always clean, and everything is kept in order and manicured. Why? Because their souls have arrived at a level where chaos, disorder, and filth cannot co-exist. It irritates them.

If you notice where the poor people live? Trash, filth, dirt, loud music, and chaos will be everywhere. They are all human souls, but with different mind-sets and in different stages of life. They need to be trained and empowered to reach self-awareness. The purpose of empowerment is to bring them to self-awareness.

Know that most of those rich people were poor at some point. They or someone in their past generation decided to turn things around. Because they came to self-awareness, which led to self-discovery, which led to self-empowerment, which led to self-actualization. Now their posterity is enjoying the benefits of their decisions and hard work. This is why Kingdom Education is important.

Self-awareness occurs when an individual finds the answers to the three age-old questions of *Who am I? Where did I come from? Why am I here?* This should be the purpose of all education—to help each individual find these answers.

The first two questions have to do with self-awareness. The third question has to do with self-discovery. When an individual finds the answers to those questions, they are ready to live.

Kings and Priests

The Bible says we are all kings and priests or a royal priesthood (1 Peter 2:9) in God's kingdom. Each individual is a king in God's kingdom. Kings have dominions or kingdoms.

If everyone is a king, then how do we all rule or have dominion at the same time? We do this by fulfilling our respective and individual callings.

When we think of kings, we think of palaces, thrones, armies, and servants. This is not how kings function in God's kingdom. That is the gentile form of kingdom and rulership.

In God's kingdom we *rule* by serving others with our gifts and skills, and by solving their problems. This is how Jesus, the King of kings, showed us how to do it.

When you master a gift or a skill, and use these, you will become a *king* over that aspect or area of life, which will in turn, creates influence. To the extent that influence reaches, is the *territory* which that individual needs to occupy and rule for God's kingdom in this life. This is how we exercise our dominion mandate on the earth.

To the extent of the territory our influence reaches is the territory we occupy for God's kingdom. That is our dominion and that which gives us jurisdiction over that territory. It could be physical (geographical), spiritual, or intellectual (occupying people's mind) territories.

Then, it is our responsibility to make sure only God's will is accomplished in the territory we occupy. That is how some people in our day are known or called *king of this* or *king of that*! It means they have mastered a skill or a gift, and took dominion over it, and became a king in that area.

We shouldn't allow any *serpents* to come into the territory we occupy. Then, before we leave, we need to hand over that territory to the next generation; and they should be prepared to take it to the next level and extend it, by fulfilling their calling.

When each believer fulfills their calling in this manner, there won't be any room left for the enemy to operate in. This is how we will occupy the entire earth for God's kingdom. This is what God is waiting for.

There is only one King of kings in God's kingdom. It is not any president or prime minister or any other royalty. That King is Jesus Christ. We are all royalty and ministers in the kingdom of God, because we are all kings and priests.

Healing of the Nations

Nations are in need of healing. Because every nation is made of people who have not gone through the stages mentioned in this book, they feel trapped and enslaved by the systems and religions of this world.

They are living a fake life based on a false identity. For that reason, nothing is working the way it is supposed to work. Life is miserable for the most part. They are hanging in there because they have to or for their family's sake.

Our hospitals are filled with patients. Most of the diseases and sicknesses are rooted in emotional or spiritual causes. Medicine alone cannot cure these precious souls. They need a different type of treatment and cure.

Our governments, economy, educational system, agriculture, ecosystem, healthcare system, family life are all *sick*; which means they are not functioning as they should. There is enough money and food for everyone; and so, no one needs to live in hunger, poverty, or in debt.

First of all we need to find out what made human beings sick in the beginning.

The Story of Three Trees

We became emotionally and spiritually sick by eating the fruit of a tree called the Knowledge of Good and Evil. That's where all the trouble began.

What is going to heal us and the nations is not more sophisticated hospitals and more medications, NGOs, or any new type of governments, or more weapons of mass destruction.

We need to be delivered from that fruit and the effects which the Tree of the Knowledge of Good and Evil brought about in our life and on the earth.

The Bible says what is going to heal the nations are the fruits and leaves of a different tree. This may surprise and shock you. How can a tree heal the nations? Because it was a tree and its fruit that made us all sick.

The entire life on earth is the story of three trees.

Two trees were in the Garden of Eden—the Tree of the Knowledge of Good and Evil, and the Tree of Life. When Adam and Eve ate the fruit of the wrong tree, God prevented them from eating from the Tree of Life. He removed them from the Garden and blocked the entrance, by appointing Cherubim to guard it.

We shouldn't eat from the Tree of Life while we have the effects and systems in us that were activated by eating from the wrong tree—It will be counterproductive.

First, we must get rid of the wrong one.

God knew the solution isn't allowing us back into the Garden and eating from the Tree of Life. Rather, before He could do this for us, He had to deliver us from the fruit of the Knowledge of Good and Evil and the consequences it brought upon humanity. To accomplish this, He decided to introduce a third tree.

That *tree* is *the cross* on which Jesus was crucified. Jesus died on the cross for the sins of the whole world.

What was the original sin from which all other sin came from? The original sin was eating from the wrong tree and the consequences it brought upon humanity and the earth.

The third three or the cross delivers us from this, and opens the door back to Eden (kingdom of God) and the Tree of Life.

In the last chapter of the Bible, we read about what is going to heal the nations:

> ***In the middle of its street, and on either side of the river, was the tree of life, which bore twelve fruits, each tree yielding its fruit every month. The leaves of the tree were for the healing of the nations. And there shall be no more curse.*** – Revelation 22:2b-3a

Concluding Thoughts

When a person goes through the process mentioned in this book that person will begin to get healed from within and become whole in their spirit, soul, and then eventually their body.

When we are whole, then we can help others, and help our community, nation; and then the whole creation, to be healed. Slowly but surely, nations will start healing from all of their *diseases* and dysfunctions from within. Every social, political, economic, and religious *disease, divisions, and crises* that are killing people and destroying our planet; will start to heal and disappear.

> ***And God will wipe away every tear from their eyes; there shall be no more death, nor sorrow, nor crying. There shall be no more pain, for the former things have passed away.*** – Revelation 21:4

Life will start to manifest on earth as it should have been. The Kingdom of heaven will be established on the earth. Human beings and the Earth will realign with heaven once again. This is why the *Tree of Life Project* is so important.

Nations are perishing and governments are running out of solutions and resources. Most governments are running on borrowed money. The next step for some governments would be to take the extreme step of starting to kill its citizens. Which has happened before several times in history. This should never happen again.

I am prompted by the King to give this book for free to anyone who wants to read it. This book is far too precious to sell for a few dollars. It is too costly for anyone not to have it. This book might save their lives.

Don't just read this book once and then put it aside. Interact with it, by answering the questionnaires. This is a great tool to read and study together as a family or a group, and track the progress.

What I am asking is, if you are blessed and impacted by reading this book; out of your gratefulness, you are more than welcome to send a donation to the **Tree of Life Project** which we are happening across the globe. Your donation will help us to print more copies of this book to give these out to people everywhere.

This is a huge project, and it will not end until everyone on earth is reached by this message, and all the nations are healed and restored.

Chapter 7 | Self-Government

There is much more to know about those two trees that were in the Garden of Eden and why God put them there. For example: What do the twelve fruits and leaves of the Tree of Life represent?

This book is not about that. There are other resources that are available to study deeper about these things. If you are interested, you may order *The Birthing of a Kingdom Nation* and *What Happened to God* books.

If you are blessed by reading this book, share it with others. Send it as a gift to your friends and families. For printed copies, all you have to pay is the shipping.

Thank you so much for being part of the **Tree of Life**. I would encourage you to form communities and groups, and go through this book together.

I encourage you to join the **Healing of the Nations Movement**. The healing of the nations cannot happen without your personal involvement. Please don't think that you don't have much to offer. However small you may think, the little that you have plays a huge role in someone else's life. They are waiting for you.

For the next step please visit www.Treeof-life.com website and follow the instructions given there.

To know more about God's kingdom and His government please read *The Birthing of a Kingdom Nation* **and** *What Happened to God* **books. To order a copy of each, visit www.TheKingdomNetwork.org**

Reflection and Action

What areas of your life still rely on external motivation instead of inner conviction and alignment with God's Spirit?

_____

_____

_____

_____

What mind-set shifts do you need to make in order to live as someone truly governed by the Spirit, not the flesh or external systems?

_____

_____

_____

_____

What need in your surroundings may be waiting for you to act with what God has already given you?

_____

_____

_____

_____

Is your influence expanding God's Kingdom, or merely maintaining your comfort or status?

_____

Principles of Self Governance

Do you see yourself as a Kingdom ambassador—bringing Heaven to Earth, or just a spectator within the systems of this world?

In what areas of your life have you been eating from the "Tree of the Knowledge of Good and Evil"—living by performance, judgment, fear, or control?

"Healing the Nations begins with me." Do you believe this is true in your life? If so, what would it require of you today?

Proposal to all Visionaries

Prepared for Anyone Who Wants to Make a Difference

Prepared by: *The Tree of Life Organization*

Introductory Remarks

Dear Revolutionary,

> Thank you for reading the *Principles of Self-Governance* book. We hope you have been deeply touched by it. Now let's start the journey of transformation.
>
> Once you finish reading the book and go through the process presented in the Tree of Life Website, it is time for you to share this with your friends and family.
>
> Once they finish reading and go through the same process, then come together as a team to prepare a project plan to tackle a need or crisis your community or nation is facing. Your team will be the *Agents of Healing and Transformation* in your community.

Principles of Self Governance

You are not alone in this. The Tree of Life team is here to help you with every step of the process. We believe you have been chosen and positioned for this very moment—when the future of your country, and even the world, stands at a crossroads. We honor your sacrifice and the great weight you carry as you are part of this *Healing of the Nations* movement.

As you work tirelessly to fulfill the vision of your life, church, business or organization, we come alongside you with this proposal—a system, and a process that will not only support the incredible work you are doing, but secure its legacy for generations to come.

This is more than a strategy. It is a spiritual and moral reset for us individually—a blueprint for lasting transformation for our community. .

We humbly offer you this proposal: a personal and national framework of Self-Governance that addresses the root causes of crises and offers a pathway to solutions, peace, unity, and national healing which would enable us to see the fulfillment of our dreams and visions that the Lord has put in each one of our hearts.

Executive Summary

This proposal outlines a national strategy rooted in the ancient but practical model of Self-Governance to address the most urgent political, economic, social, and religious crises. It is based on a historical fact: systems built on external control and fear will eventually collapse.

The long-term solution lies not in more laws or external enforcement, but in empowering citizens to govern themselves from within—spiritually, morally, emotionally, and intellectually.

Chapter 7 | Self-Government

The following framework offers a five-stage personal and social development model—*Self-Awareness, Self-Discovery, Self-Empowerment, Self-Actualization,* and *Self-Governance*—which will first lead to individual transformation, and then a national one, and a global one. We believe this system, if piloted and scaled, can:

- Reduce poverty and unemployment
- Reduce crime and division
- Restore national unity
- Eliminate dependency-based programs
- Drastically reduce government spending
- Revive the educational, healthcare, and economic systems
- Transform your country, into a global example of peace and sustainability

Background and Problem Statement

Despite massive spending, policy revisions, and military investment, international conflicts, and issues such as illegal immigration, economic instability, political polarization, social unrest, mental health crises, and educational system failure continue to escalate.

The current model is reactive, not transformational. As such, its efforts focus on symptoms rather than the roots: broken identity, loss of purpose, and the widespread adoption of false or externally imposed identities.

The challenge is not a lack of resources but a lack of cohesive vision and alignment between spirit, character, purpose, and leadership at the individual and national levels.

Proposed Solution: The Self-Governance National Framework

We propose a phased, cross-sectoral implementation of the Self-Governance model beginning with six core pillars:

1. A National Self-Awareness and Identity Initiative

This involves the following:

- Educational programs and media campaigns to teach the principles of authentic identity, purpose, and value beyond race, gender, profession, or political affiliation.

- A curriculum integrated into schools, to help children answer the fundamental questions: Who am I? Where did I come from? Why am I here?

2. Transformational Education Reform

This entails the following:

- Replace outdated, performance-based systems with value and merit-based education rooted in purpose and emotional intelligence.

- Focus on discovery and mastery of natural talents, character-building, and community contribution.

- Engage retired educators and local leaders in implementing community learning centers.

3. Holistic Health and Wellness System

This is achieved by the following:

- Address root causes of illness by focusing on emotional and spiritual health as the foundation of physical well-being.

- Encourage natural food production systems, family-based healing, and emotional resilience training in schools and communities.

- Phase out profit-driven models in favor of wellness-driven systems.

4. Immigration and Refugee Integration Program

If applicable, this will involve:

- Vetting + Orientation model: Every immigrant receives language education, values training, civic education, and support for purposeful integration.

- Providing vocational training and purpose discovery programs to turn "burdens" into builders.

5. Economic Revitalization through Self-Empowerment

This will entail:

- Training youth in financial literacy, entrepreneurship, and resource stewardship from an early age.

- Helping citizens break the cycle of consumer and debt-driven poverty and embrace creativity, productivity, and purpose-aligned work.

6. Localized Governance Structures

The structures envisioned, include the following:

- Establish City Elders Councils—teams of respected local leaders to serve as moral gatekeepers and community shepherds.

- Equip law enforcement, not only to maintain order, but to support the self-governance transformation at the neighborhood level.

Implementation Plan

Phase 1 Development & Preparation (6–8 months):

- Form a planning council composed of educators, spiritual leaders, psychologists, economists, and administrators.

- Secure funding, land, and logistical support for pilot campuses.

- Develop a full curriculum, training materials, assessing and vetting systems.

Phase 2 Pilot Programs (Year 1–2):

- Launch in 3–5 towns or key cities as demonstration zones.

- Document transformation data in schools, prisons, immigrant communities, and economic output.

Phase 3 National Rollout (Year 3–5):

- Federal adoption of revised curricula and standards.

- Scale the model across all states and provinces.

- Begin global outreach to export the model of peace and purpose-led prosperity.

Funding Request to the Government

Once you have the detailed plan regarding any particular issue or crisis and a community that is ready for action, feel free to present a proposal to your local or Federal government for a funding request. We respectfully request a fraction of the funds currently allocated to military expansion, or inefficient welfare programs in order to build the infrastructure and pilot programs for this initiative.

A specific budget will be presented upon further consultation, but the total investment would be negligible compared to existing national expenditures—with the potential for billions in long-term savings.

Expected Outcomes

Within 5–7 years, the following outcomes can be expected:

- Crime rates drop significantly
- Prison populations decline
- Immigration becomes manageable and productive
- Health and wellness improve across demographics
- Economic productivity increases through empowered citizens
- A restored sense of national unity and spiritual health
- Your town or nation becomes a prototype nation—a global beacon of hope

Closing Remarks

We are living in a moment unlike any other—a golden window of opportunity to heal our land and lead the world into a new era of peace, purpose, and prosperity.

What you are doing today is setting the pace for the next thousand years. However, for this change to be complete and enduring, we must also transform from within—spiritually, emotionally, and morally.

We ask you for the opportunity to share this book and present this plan to your friends, and to anyone who is interested in making a difference. What we are proposing is not theory—it is a tested truth.

So, give us the people no one wants. Give us the broken systems, the forgotten communities, and the confused youth. We will turn them into a generation of heroes.

We believe the Tree of Life Self-Governance framework can eliminate crime, poverty, division, and debt—restoring nations as the beacon of hope and light for the entire world.

You have the chance to be remembered as one of the most influential leaders in modern history—not through might, but through moral and spiritual awakening.

Together, we can transform and heal our nations, not just for this generation, but for many generations to come.

With deepest respect, prayer, and unwavering commitment,

The Tree of Life Organization

Bibliography and Recommended Resources

Discipling Nations Series

Kingdom Mandate (for any donation)
Discovering the Lost Kingdom (Volume 1) $14.00
Purpose, Calling, and Gifts (Volume 2) $15.00
God's Original Design (Volume 3) $20.00
Seeing, Entering, and Manifesting the Kingdom of God (Volume 4)$20.00
The Ekklesia (Volume 5) $30.00
The Gospel of the Kingdom (Volume 6) $20.00
Power and Authority of the Church (Volume 7) $15.00
Kingdom Family (Volume 8) $15.00
The Birthing of a Kingdom Nation (Volume 9) $20.00
What Happened to God? (Volume10) $20.00
7 Dimensions and Operations of the Kingdom of God (Volume 11) $15.00
Kingdom Economy (Volume 12) $15.00
Kingdom Government (Volume 13) $15.00
Releasing Kings and Queens to their Original Intent (Volume 14) $10.00
Kingdom Secrets to Restoring Nations Back to God (Volume 15) $20.00
Keys to Fulfilling Your Kingdom Assignment (Volume 16) $15.00

Kingdom Living Series

The Three Most Important Decisions of Your Life $15.00
Recognizing God's Timing for Your Life $12.00
Overcoming the Spirit of Poverty $10.00
Seven Kinds of Believers $10.00
7 Dimensions of God's Glory $5.00
7 Dimensions of God's Grace $10.00
7 Kinds of Faith $7.00

Kingdom Books for Kids

Genesis 126 Three Volume Book set for boys $25.00

To place an order:

www.TheKingdomNetwork.org
Phone: 1-800-558-5020
Email: info@TheKingdomNetwork.org

Brief psychotic disorder. Lexicon of Psychology: Glossary / Lexicon. 16/04/2025. https://www.psychology-lexicon.com/cms/glossary/5-glossary-b/3984-brief-psychotic-disorder.html?highlight=WyJwc3l-jaG90aWMiXQ==

Duke University study by Dr. Wendy Wood. Published as *"Habits in Everyday Life: Thought, Emotion, and Action."* Wood, W., Quinn, J. M., & Kashy, D. A. (2002). Journal of Personality and Social Psychology, 83(6), 1281–1297.

Are you struggling to discover your **PURPOSE** ?
You are not supposed to fit in but stand out !

Sign up today for the FREE Online Kingdom Course

DISCOVERING

THE LOST KINGDOM

In this course you'll DISCOVER:

>> Your true identity and purpose
>> What God is doing on the earth and how you can partner with Him in it
>> Why God created the earth and put us on this planet
>> And much more ...

Why are people becoming more and more disinterested in **church and religion** globally?
Join the course, and discover
what your soul has been searching for all along.

FREE
BOOK AND
STUDY GUIDE

Other courses available
>> DISCOVERING PURPOSE, CALLING AND GIFTS
>> SEEING, ENTERING AND MANIFESTING THE KINGDOM
>> GOD'S ORIGINAL DESIGN
>> The Ekklesia
>> The Next move of GOD
   And more ...

Register Now @ **www.TheKingdomUniversity.org**

Welcome to
KINGDOM DELIVERANCE
— WORKSHOP —

Are you tired of waiting and looking for breakthroughs? Kingdom of God has the answer.

This kingdom deconstruct workshop is divided into EIGHT major categories which deal with the eight major areas of our life. Each one is connected to the next, and so if one of these areas dysfunctions, it will affect all other areas of your life.

1. Relationship with the Father
2. Spiritual Healing
3. Emotional Healing
4. Recognizing Purpose and Calling
5. Identifying and Mastering Natural and Spiritual Gifts
6. Finances—Learning to Live in Kingdom Economy
7. Healing Relationships
8. Physical Health

Take action now. Order all 8 workshop manuals today !

Thank you so much for taking the courses from The Kingdom University. Taking a course is only the first step. We are pleased to present you with the next step—that of going through the process to get rid of all the extra weights that have been slowing and hindering you from fully living out your kingdom assignment.

Call 1 800 558 5020   www.TheKingdomNetwork.org

www.ingramcontent.com/pod-product-compliance
Lightning Source LLC
Chambersburg PA
CBHW070141080526
44586CB00015B/1795